WONDER STRUCK

AWAKEN TO THE NEARNESS *of* GOD

MARGARET FEINBERG

LIFEWAY PRESS®
NASHVILLE, TENNESSEE

Published by LifeWay Press®

Second printing 2013

ISBN: 978-1-4158-7420-2

Item: 005515743

Dewey Decimal Classification Number: 248.84

Subject Headings: CHRISTIAN LIFE \ GOD–LOVE \ HOPE

Printed in the United States of America

Adult Ministry Publishing

LifeWay Church Resources

One LifeWay Plaza

Nashville, Tennessee 37234-0152

We believe that the Bible has God for its author; salvation for its end; and truth, without any mixture of error, for its matter and that all Scripture is totally true and trustworthy. To review LifeWay's doctrinal guideline, please visit *www.lifeway.com/doctrinalguideline.*

TABLE OF CONTENTS

MEET THE AUTHOR
MARGARET FEINBERG

Margaret Feinberg is a popular Bible teacher and speaker at churches and leading conferences such as Catalyst, Thrive, and Extraordinary Women. Her books and Bible studies have sold over 600,000 copies and received critical acclaim and extensive national media coverage from CNN, the Associated Press, *USA Today, Los Angeles Times, Washington Post,* and many others.

She was recently named one of 50 Women to Watch by *Christianity Today,* one of the 30 Voices who will help lead the church in the next decade by *Charisma* magazine, and one of the '40 Under 40' who will shape Christian publishing by *Christian Retailing* magazine. Margaret currently lives in Morrison, Colorado, with her husband, Leif and their superpup, Hershey.

One of her greatest joys is hearing from her readers. Go ahead, become her friend on Facebook, follow her on Twitter or Pinterest @mafeinberg, or check out her website at *www.margaretfeinberg.com.*

DEAR LEADER,

I WANT TO BEGIN by giving you a big bear hug, looking deep into your eyes, and saying thank you. Thank you for taking the time to lead participants through this study called *Wonderstruck*. I know your time and energy are pulled in many different directions, and I want to begin by thanking you for your willingness to sacrifice to draw others closer to Christ. I'm grateful for you. I can't wait to hear what our Abba Father is going to do in and through you and your group in the weeks ahead.

You also need to know that I've been praying for you. I've asked God to speak to, lead, guide, encourage, and infuse you with more of His presence. I pray that in the moments you're tempted to believe you have to have all the right answers, the Holy Spirit will gently remind you that what's often most needed is a warm smile, a readiness to pray, and an offer to grab coffee together and allow the person to talk.

I've also asked God that over the upcoming weeks you won't just help others discover the wonder of God, but you would be wonderstruck, too. If you'll drop us a note at *wonderstruck@margaretfeinberg.com* and let us know when your group is meeting, we want to pray for you and your participants during this time. Oh! And if you have any questions along the way, feel free to send those, too.

Thank you, my friend, for being courageous enough to lead others Christward. I can't wait to meet you and give you that bear hug in person. May you be wonderstruck and live even more awake and aware to the wonder of God all around.

BLESSINGS,

MARGARET

This study invites you deeper into the trade book *Wonderstruck*. You can participate in the study without the trade book, but you'll get more out of the experience if you pick up a copy—(available in paperback, electronic, and audiobook formats).

LEADER'S GUIDE

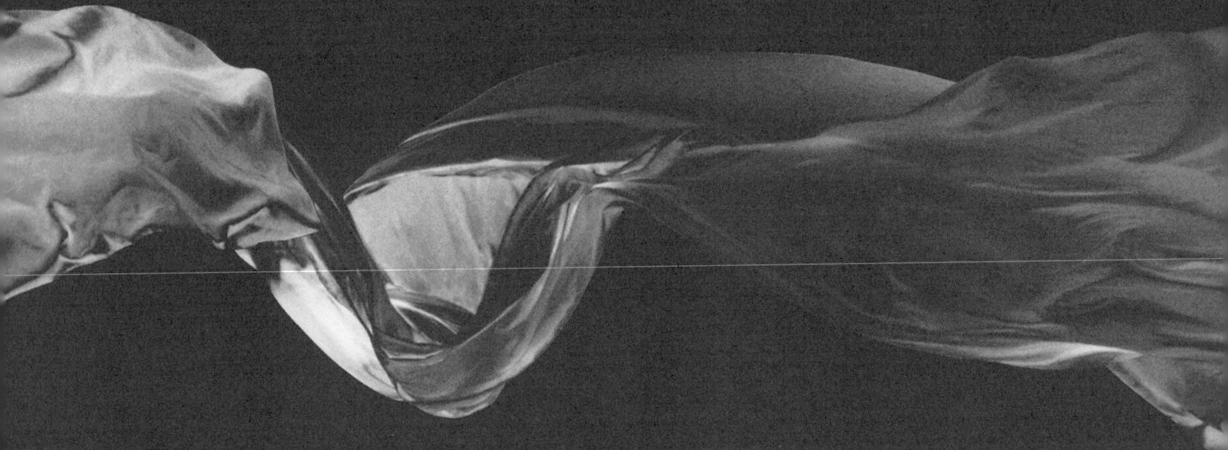

THIS BRIEF LEADER'S GUIDE is designed to help you take participants through this book and Bible study. As you prepare for this study, go ahead and watch several sessions ahead of time so that you'll have a feel for the study's direction.

In the Leader's Kit, you'll find a copy of the *Wonderstruck* tradebook. Reading the book in advance will help you prepare for leading the study and provide you with additional insights and background. The book is not required for participants, but after reading, you may want to recommend group members pick up an electronic, audiobook, or paperback copy to get the most out of the experience.

As you prepare for each session, here's a basic outline of what to expect:

EXPERIENTIAL ACTIVITY

Depending on the amount of time you have to meet together and the resources available, you'll want to begin the session with the experiential activity. You will find these activities on the group page that begins each week. This interactive icebreaker is designed to be a trigger for group engagement as well as move people toward the ideas explored in the teaching. You'll always want to read ahead to the following week's activity to see what's needed and how participants may be able to contribute.

HOMEWORK GROUP DISCUSSION

Next in each lesson (with the exception of the first and last) you will lead the group to review the homework from the previous week. Encourage participants to share what they're learning and how the Holy Spirit is at work in their lives.

PLAY SESSION VIDEO

After you've finished the homework discussion, it's time to play the video. The teaching presentations will range from 20-30 minutes.

NOTES

Encourage participants to take notes as they watch the video.

VIDEO DISCUSSION

Dive into the video discussion questions next. Based on the amount of time your group meets, you may need to prayerfully determine which questions are best suited for your group and their needs. Don't feel as though you need to ask every question. Rely on the Holy Spirit for guidance on any additional questions or follow-up that needs to be asked as the discussion progresses.

CLOSING PRAYER

Always save time for prayer before you close. Ask the Holy Spirit to open everyone's eyes and hearts to the wonder of God all around.

Thank you, again, for leading this Bible study. I pray that you experience the wonder of God in amazing ways.

THE WONDER OF DIVINE EXPECTATION

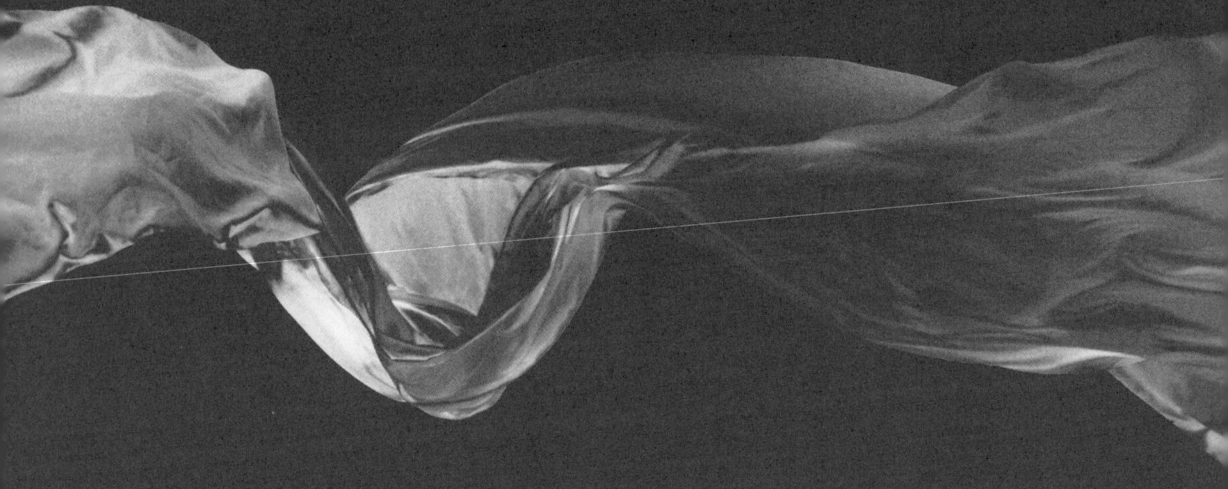

SESSION ONE

GROUP GETTING STARTED: (10-15 minutes)

SESSION ONE: THE WONDER OF DIVINE EXPECTATION

EXPERIENTIAL ACTIVITY: RECOGNIZE THE WONDER OF GOD IN OUR LIVES

WHAT YOU'LL NEED:

- Two balloons for each participant
- A black marker for each participant
- A small pin or thumbtack

1 Blow up the balloons ahead of time (consider using a small pump) or purchase helium filled balloons.

2 Ask participants to write what takes away the wonder of God in their life the most on one balloon (e.g. busyness, responsibility).

3 Ask each participant to write what in the last week has renewed their sense of the wonder of God on the second balloon (e.g. birth of a baby, renewal of a friendship, walk through a forest, moment in Scripture).

4 Invite each participant to share what they've written on their balloons. After they share what takes away from their sense of wonder, invite them to pop the first balloon so they're left holding the balloon that awakens the wonder of God.

5 Discuss the following questions:

Do you tend to focus more of your energy on what takes away from the wonder of God or what awakens the sense of wonder in your life? Why?

What can you do to nurture a sense of wonder as represented by your balloon?

PLAY THE SESSION ONE VIDEO: [23:15]

NOTES

____

____

____

____

____

VIDEO DISCUSSION

1 Turn to page 162. Over the next six weeks, you'll be challenged to awaken even more to the presence of God in your life. One of the ways to do this is to make daily entries into the Wonderstruck Journal. On page 163, begin today by listing three moments in which you've encountered the wonder of God and His handiwork. Note your first three entries and share them with the group.

2 Which name of God listed in Isaiah 9:6 is most familiar to you in your spiritual journey? Which is least familiar? Explain.

3 Why do you think God reveals His name as Wonderful? What do you think is communicated about the nature and character of God through this title?

4 Invite a participant to read Psalm 77:11 aloud. When was the last time you found yourself taken back by the wonder of God? What did you learn about the character or nature of God through the experience?

5 What disappointments or letdowns from the past or present tend to dampen any sense of divine expectation in your life?

6 What are you currently doing to nurture a sense of divine expectation?

CLOSING PRAYER

As you close in prayer ask:

- God to awaken each person's heart, mind, and spirit to a sense of God's wonder
- God to grant participants a renewed sense of divine expectation in their lives
- the Holy Spirit to orchestrate divine opportunities over the upcoming weeks to experience God's presence and grow closer to Him.

DAY ONE

AWAKE TO WONDER

I NEVER EXPECTED TO FIND love in Alaska. I only travelled to the tiny town of Sitka to help my aunt with her bed and breakfast. But during one stay, I fell head over heels for a six-foot-eight local guy named Leif (pronounced Lay-f). Norwegian by descent, Leif and I were married just a little over a year after we first met. For the first five years of our marriage, we lived in Alaska. During that time I had the privilege of seeing the Northern Lights on countless evenings. But one night stood out above the rest.

THIS WEEK:

If you are following along in the trade book, read chapters ".000: Captured by the Night Sky" and ".001: Hidden Among the Highlands" and tackle the five days of homework to prepare for the next gathering.

While taking an overnight ferry from Sitka to Juneau, I remember admiring the faint moonlight backlighting the mountainous coast. Then something compelled me to look up, and a scene unfolded that I suspect caused at least one angel to gasp: The expanse of the sky transformed from inky blackness into an infinite canvas on which brushstrokes of apricot, sapphire, and emerald were painted into the night sky.

BONUS ACTIVITY:

To see some breathtaking images of the Northern Lights or Aurora Borealis, search Google for "Images of Northern Lights."

The hours passed. In the wake of such beauty, I offered up a silent prayer to lay hold of the wonder of God, to find myself once again awed by another facet of His nature, another glimpse of His presence in our world. God desires to captivate us not just with His handiwork but with Himself—displaying facets of His character, igniting us with His fiery love, awakening us to the intensity of His holiness.

Often such incidents occur when we least anticipate, leaving us wonderstruck much like my encounter with the Northern Lights. But we can live each day trusting that the God who met us in the past will once again greet us with arms wide open in the future.

God extends uncounted invitations to encounter Him, yet too often I sleep straight through. Unconscious of the life God desires for me, I slumber in the presence of the sacred and snore in the company of the divine. Inactive and inert, I become a spiritual sleepyhead who clamors for the snooze button rather than climbing out of bed.

God is busting at the seams to display His glory, His power, and His might in a way that leaves us awestruck, breathless, and wide awake

BONUS ACTIVITY:

Spend time committing Psalm 77:11 to memory this week. You'll find a flash card on page 177.

to His presence in our world. God longs for us to live awake to Him and all that He is doing in our world. Indeed, our God is Wonderful.

What three words come to mind when you think of "wonder"?

The dictionary defines wonder as being filled with "admiration, amazement, or awe; marvel."[1]

In so many ways, those are the fruits of life with God. We are created to live in such a way that our lives are acts of worship where we express our adoration, affection, and appreciation of God at every turn. The presence of God and His work in our world should leave us awestruck. Now let me be clear: Experiencing the wonder of God isn't about landing a crazy story to tell our friends or experiencing pimply goose bumps. The wonder awakens us to dive even deeper in our relationship with God.

That's why I define the wonder of God as the following:

THE WONDER OF GOD: A MOMENT OF SPIRITUAL AWAKENING THAT MAKES US CURIOUS TO KNOW GOD MORE.

Reflecting on this definition, when was the last time you encountered the wonder of God?

The wonder of God stirs our spiritual longings and makes us hungry for God in ways that often lead us into moments of transformation. Our eyes open. Our ears hear. Our hearts soften in the presence of God. Our wills more readily yield to God. Our worship becomes more pleasing to God.

What are the two components of acceptable worship mentioned in Hebrews 12:28-29?

+ BONUS ACTIVITY:

Rich Hammar captures astrophotography images from his driveway in Springfield, Missouri, using specialized equipment. Some of his images have been featured on NASA's homepage. Check out *www.seetheglory.com.*

If I'm honest with you, despite the breathtaking and transformative moments of God that I've experienced, all too often I find myself like so many of the other passengers on the ferry that evening in Alaska—deep in sleep, missing the moment. I succumb to spiritual weariness rather than remaining alert to the wondrous displays that reveal more of God. In those moments, the burning bushes in my life are reduced to smoldering distractions, and the still small voice becomes something I absentmindedly shush.

What are the wonders of God you've taken for granted rather than responding with awe?

On the continuum below, mark how often you pass by God's presence and handiwork unaware:

I often pass by God's presence and handiwork unaware. ———— I rarely pass by God's presence and handiwork unaware.

How do you think you can become more aware and awake to the wonders of God?

NOTABLE:

The wonders that I fail to marvel can be as simple as the gift of each day, the beauty of creation, the delight of God's Word, or the compassion of a friend.

For me, becoming more aware of the wonder of God in my life began with a simple request: I prayed for wonder. To this day, I stand in awe of the ways God has answered—as you'll discover in the weeks ahead.

That's why I'd like to invite you to offer up a similar prayer. Will you pray for wonder right now? Ask God to awaken your ability to see and savor His sweet presence and recognize His divine handiwork.

Then live eyes wide open to the ways God answers.

One great way to live expectant for God is keep a wonder journal. During the opening session, you were asked to write down three of God's wonders you've experienced. Will you commit to write down three items each day?

CLOSING PRAYER: Spend time praying that you'll be wonderstruck. With each passing page and session, ask God to help you discover another facet of His character, feel the soft pinch of His presence, and step back in astonishment of the One who holds everything together.

DAY TWO

EXPECT THE UNEXPECTED

ONE OF THE GREAT THINGS we can expect of God is the unexpected. By His nature, God's ways are so much more vibrant, breathtaking, and all encompassing than our own. This is one of the most exciting aspects of living with divine expectation: We can lean into the idea that whatever God has up His sleeve is better than anything we could imagine on our own.

What ignites in you the desire to live with a holy anticipation that God wants to meet you?

As I've been praying for wonder, I've been asking God to infuse me with the Holy Spirit so that I'm more sensitive to His nudging and leading. I hope you are, too. I've been living in awe of the unexpected ways God answers.

QUOTABLE:

"I want the presence of God Himself, or I don't want anything at all to do with religion. I want all that God has or I don't want any." –A.W. Tozer, author and pastor

On the continuum below, mark how often you tend to live with a sense of divine expectation:

I don't live with any sense of divine expectation.	I live wildly expectant of God to do great things.

What prevents you from living with the expectation that God wants to do awesome work in, through, and around you as described in Exodus 34:10?

We recently traveled through Baltimore when God surprised us with an encounter. We stopped by a local grocery store to grab our favorite road travel supplies—water, fresh fruit, and baked potato chips. Walking out of the grocery store, my husband, Leif, and I saw a woman on her cell phone with three kids in tow. She complained that there weren't enough beds to serve the homeless women in need in the city. We looked at each other, unsure of the best way to respond, and returned to the car.

Then we noticed a quick eats restaurant in the strip mall and decided to grab a meal. As we waited to order, we discussed what we just saw.

"Was it real or a con?" we debated. Yep. We're guilty of watching one too many episodes of *Dateline,* too. The situation seemed a little too perfect.

On her cell phone. Talking loudly. Outside a busy grocery store.

When was the last time you second-guessed a person's motives in asking for help?

How do you handle situations like this?

Before eating, we prayed and waited for a sense of the best way to respond.

Then. She appeared. Again.

She brought her three kids into the eatery to use the restroom.

Leif and I debated how to assist her and if we were the ones to help. Neither of us had a tremendous sense of peace about what to do or how to do it. The parable of the man whose body was left for dead along the road came to mind. I calculated dozens of reasons not to help the woman—including getting conned.

Make a list of five reasonable explanations for not helping the man left for dead along the road in Luke 10:29-37.

The priest and Levite (temple worker) in this story aren't doing something their contemporaries would consider wrong. Avoiding the beaten man on the road was following God's law. If the man was dead and they touched him, or if he died in their arms, they wouldn't be able to do their job for seven days. These two men choose to follow the purity law, but ignore the law about loving their neighbor. They consciously decide that the beaten man must not be their neighbor and move along.

Yet the Samaritan man is the one who reverses the robbers' actions. While the robbers took money, the Samaritan gave. The robbers beat, the Samaritan bandaged. The robbers left the man for dead and never returned; the Samaritan left the man in the care of the innkeeper and promised to return.

NOTABLE:

The 17-mile journey from Jerusalem down to Jericho is known as "The Bloody Way." The elevation drops from 2,500 feet above sea level to 825 feet below sea level. Walking the windy, steep, rocky road would be similar to walking in a dangerous alley in a big city with money dangling out of your pockets.

Something inside reminded me that showing compassion was worth the risk of being conned.

Leif pulled out cash and asked, "How much should we give her?"

A number came to mind.

Walking out of the restaurant, we saw the woman walking into the liquor store down the strip mall. Again, Leif and I looked at each other, second-guessing that maybe this wasn't such a good idea.

She emerged without a purchase.

I took a gulp and walked toward her.

"What is this?" she asked as I shoved the money into her hand.

"Cash," I said. "Bless you!"

"Who are you—an angel?" she asked, welling up with tears.

"No," I smiled and started to turn away.

"Wait!" she yelled. Then the woman pointed to her son and explained that the boy had autism. "But he knows how to love. Can he give you a hug?"

QUOTABLE:

"Who among the gods is like you, LORD? Who is like you—majestic in holiness, awesome in glory, working wonders?" –Exodus 15:11

This boy wrapped his arms around me, my face squished in the nape of his neck, and I knew I'd encountered the wonder of God.

Driving away, Leif and I prayed for this woman and her children. I was so grateful for the opportunity to be a conduit of God's goodness, but I never expected to receive such a gift, a pure expression of love from a child, in return. Sometimes we have to take risks, including getting conned, to be wonderstruck by the love of God.

When have you seen God answer the prayer of Psalm 17:7 in your life? Spend a few moments asking God to reveal this wonder in greater measure.

What stops you from taking bigger risks in your walk with God?

When have you taken a risk and been wonderstruck by God through the process?

My hope for you is that you'll take big risks in order to reach out to others and share God's love with them. Not every story will end like you hope, but along the way you're going to encounter our God, who is full of wonders, in unexpected ways.

CLOSING PRAYER: Spend some time asking God to raise the level of divine expectation in your life and expect the unexpected. Ask God to place people in your life over the course of the next week on whom you can lavish the love of God.

DAY THREE

WONDERSTRUCK BY A GLIMPSE OF GOD

WHEN WAS THE LAST TIME YOU found yourself taken back by the wonder of God? If you spend time reflecting on who God is and all that He's done, it's hard not to be caught up in the wonder.

Take a few moments and reflect on the some of the characteristics of God listed below:

WISE	MERCIFUL	MAJESTIC
TRUTHFUL	GRACIOUS	ETERNAL
GOOD	PEACEFUL	ALL-POWERFUL
LOVING	FAITHFUL	UNCHANGING
JUST	EMINENCE	SOVEREIGN

My heart melts whenever I start thinking about the wondrous love of God. Or when I consider how many times God has extended the mercy I-so-don't-deserve, gratitude exudes from the core of my being. But when I think about God as being eternal I sometimes struggle to wrap my head, let alone my heart, around all that means.

Now some of these characteristics evoke a sense of wonder more than others—and that's OK. Every facet of God's character invites us to know more of Him.

To what characteristics of God does Isaiah 40:25-26 allude? Which provide you with the greatest sense of wonder?

As we pray for wonder each day, we need to live expectant for the ways God wants to reveal Himself even in the tiniest details of life. Our attention might be drawn to patterns and particulars in Scripture we've never seen before. Our spirits may waken to prayer in fresh and unexpected ways. God may choose to reveal Himself in unexpected conversations as we go through our daily life.

Here's what I've discovered: When we pray for wonder and live eyes wide open to wonder, the tone and tenacity with which we live our lives change. We become expectant to catch glimpses of God in ways we've never seen Him before.

One of my favorite places in the Bible where this occurs is in the Book of Isaiah. The death of King Uzziah ushers in an uneasy time for Judah, the Southern Kingdom. The Northern Kingdom, Israel, is about to fall to the Assyrians, leaving Judah without a buffer between the much larger enemies of the time. During this time, Isaiah's spiritual eyes are opened and he glimpses God. The Lord gives Isaiah specific instructions to speak to the people, ultimately telling them that destruction is unavoidable, but promising them that healing is coming. The scene radiates the power, wonder, and majesty of God. Yet rather than focus on the beauty or radiance of the Divine, Isaiah is reduced to describing the garnishes of the room.

NOTABLE:

During the Old Testament, God's people believed that God resided in the temple. When Isaiah glimpses God on the throne, he sees that God's robe fills the temple. God can't be confined to one location. Not even the hem of His robe fits inside.

As the holiness of God echoes throughout the chamber, even the building is not immune. The structure seizes in the wake of reverential awe and worship; smoke, a symbol of both God's acceptance and anger, fills the air. Taken back in wonder of a scene bursting with sights and smells that defy description, Isaiah only has one response: he becomes deftly aware of his own inadequacies.

Polluted. Filthy. Corrupt. Contaminated.

Though the veil is pulled back revealing all that is wonderful, Isaiah responds with the heartbreaking cry, "Woe is me!"

In a most merciful yet mysterious scene, which alludes to the coming of Christ, a burning creature removes a live coal from the altar with tongs and touches the mouth of Isaiah. The prophet's lips cauterized and purified, the seraphim announces, "Your guilt is taken away and your sin atoned for."

NOTABLE:

The name of the seraphim, which means "burning ones," suggests they're ablaze in their love of God.

NOTABLE:

Exodus 24:15-17 reminds us that God's glory and greatness cannot be measured or described. When we try to describe God in the frame of creation, we fail. But God reveals Himself as something more attainable to human understanding in Jesus Christ.

The words of the fiery angel melt me. Forgiven and cleansed, woe is replaced by wonder.

God forever ruins Isaiah. This single encounter shapes the rest of the prophet's life and message.

The encounter is stamped on Isaiah's heart, an intimate knowledge of God as "the Holy One of Israel" and becomes one of the prophet's distinctive signatures.

One glimpse of God changes everything.

Have you been transformed through encounters with God?

How were they similar to Isaiah's experience in Isaiah 6, and how were they different?

NOTABLE:

The word "holy" is repeated three times by the seraphim in verse 3. Because ancient writers didn't have punctuation or typesetting, they emphasized important points through repetition. God isn't just holy. He is the Holy of all holies.

While we may never have an encounter with God quite like Isaiah's, rest assured that God wants to meet us and give us glimpses of Himself that leave us wonderstruck and transformed. Like Isaiah, some of our encounters with God and His Word will reveal our areas of sin, leaving us with a sense of "Woe is me!"—exposing our great need for God. Other encounters will remind us of what we've been called and created to be as children of God. Still others will reveal aspects of God's character we've never considered before.

While God probably won't reveal Himself in the same way He did to Isaiah, you and I can still petition God to meet us so that we become more like Him. We can become awakened to the wonders of God all around us. As you go through this week, will you pray that God will continue to fill you with wonder? Will you note in the journal on 162 the ways He answers?

If so, your life may never be the same. You might find yourself awakened to God in ways that transform you forever.

CLOSING PRAYER: Courageously spend time in prayer asking God to ruin you with a fresh understanding of Himself. Ask God that along the way you'll find yourself awakened to facets of His character you've never seen before that will transform you forever.

DAY FOUR

WONDERSTRUCK BY THE PRAISEWORTHY DEEDS OF GOD

+ BONUS ACTIVITY:

God continually paints the skies with beauty. One of my favorite websites that captures portraits of God's handwork is *www.clouds365.com.* The award-winning site records photographs of the sky. Some of the pictures will take your breath away.

ONCE I BEGAN PRAYING FOR WONDER in my life, I began finding a sense of marvel and awe throughout the Scriptures. Not only is God full of wonders, but He displays His wonders throughout the ages. Through God's wonders people are set free, anchored deeper in their faith, and exposed to the bottomless depths of the love of God.

When we begin to pray for wonder, we need to live wide-eyed to the ways God wants to answer us. God paints facets of His handiwork and character in the sunrise and etches aspects of His nature into the canyon walls.

What are some of the ways you're beginning to experience the wonder of God as alluded to in Psalm 65:8? Don't forget to add some of your list to the Wonderstruck Journal on page 162.

God calls us not only to live wide-eyed and awake to the wonders that He is doing all around us, but to remember His wondrous works in the past. We're asked to actively remember the displays of God's faithfulness.

List the praiseworthy deeds of God in each of the following areas:

THE PRAISEWORTHY DEEDS THAT GOD
Performed in the Old Testament

1.
2.
3.
4.
5.

THE PRAISEWORTHY DEEDS THAT GOD
Performed in the New Testament
1.
2.
3.
4.
5.

THE PRAISEWORTHY DEEDS THAT GOD
Performed in My Faith Community in the Last Year
1.
2.
3.
4.
5.

THE PRAISEWORTHY DEEDS THAT GOD
Performed in My Life in the Last Year
1.
2.
3.
4.
5.

Now that you've filled in the chart, you should have a list of at least 20 ways God has revealed Himself as wonderful, not only in your life but in your church and in history. Reflecting on the list, it's hard not to be wonderstruck by God's love, intimate involvement, provision, and tender care.

One practical way to remind yourself of God's wondrous works is to make a list of His praiseworthy deeds. Why is this so important? Because unless we are intentional about remembering the deeds of God, we become forgetful about God and His presence in our world. This principle is displayed in one of the most potent psalms.

In some traditions, Psalm 78 is recited on the third through sixth days of Passover as a reminder of God's work in the lives of the Israelites from the exodus to the reign of King David. Attributed to the priests of Asaph, Psalm 78 challenges us to remember and share the wondrous work of God in our lives.

NOTABLE:

Notable: Psalm 78:9 describes the "men of Ephraim." Ephraim was one of Joseph's sons who, along with Manasseh, received land as part of the 12 tribes of Israel. Levi and Joseph did not receive tribal lands. Ephraim is another name for the Northern Kingdom or Israel.

Psalm 78 is presented as a parable or mashal, not to give chronological and accurate historical information, but to remind the Israelites about how God has worked in their lives over centuries. God's original covenant with Abraham comes to fruition despite the people's rebellion and unfaithfulness. Psalm 78 encourages readers even today to remember the active role God plays and place trust in Him.

Why is recalling and sharing God's praiseworthy deeds with others important according to Psalm 78:1-8?

NOTABLE:

Our God is an active God. Psalm 78 describes action after action of how God participated directly in the lives of the Israelites throughout history. God doesn't sit back as a spectator, but protects, saves, creates, delivers, and leads.

What can happen if we fail to recall and share these praiseworthy deeds according to Psalm 78:9-31?

Despite the people's forgetfulness and hard-heartedness, how does God continue to reveal Himself as Wonderful to the people according to Psalm 78:32-55?

What aspect or attribute of God leaves you most wonderstruck in Psalm 78:55-72?

This powerful psalm is a beautiful reminder that we need to reflect on the praiseworthy deeds of God on a regular basis. And as we remember the work of God in our lives, we can't help but live more awake to the work He wants to do.

CLOSING PRAYER: Spend some time praising God for His wondrous work in your life, family, and community. Thank God for the work He's doing around the world and the way He has shown Himself faithful throughout history.

DAY FIVE

APPREHENDED BY DIVINE AMAZEMENT

FOR ME, GROWING SLEEPY to the things of God isn't an option. I don't want a faith that's dry, boring, or feels like punching a clock. Maybe that's one reason I've been praying so persistently to be apprehended by the wonder of God. I want to be caught up in the amazement of who He is and all that He's done.

Of all the Gospel writers, I'd argue that none was caught up in the amazement of Christ as much as Luke. Now this is not to say the other authors of the Gospels weren't awestruck by Jesus. John uses the term *amazed* six times. Matthew describes people being amazed twice as much. Mark, though noted for his brevity, uses the word *amazed* 15 times. But Luke seems to be caught up in amazement at every turn.

The Greek language provides five different words that can be used to translate amazed. Luke uses all of them. In Luke 5:26, he manages to use two of them in a single verse.

The breathless excitement of Christ and all He does exudes throughout Luke's Gospel.

The wonder begins in the first chapter with the announcement of John the Baptist's birth. The miraculous circumstances of this boy's birth to a barren couple leaves everyone astonished by the wondrous display of God's power.

When have you been amazed by God's work in someone else's life like those who learned of John's birth in Luke 1:57-66?

That's just the beginning of the astonishment. The next chapter of Luke describes the birth of Jesus and His younger years. Even as a child, Jesus leaves people awestruck.

QUOTABLE:

"They were, all of them, quite simply amazed. Zechariah's friends, the shepherds, all who heard the shepherds, Joseph and Mary, the people in his hometown of Nazareth, those in Capernaum, those who heard the boy Jesus in the temple, the disciples, the parents of the girl who had died, even the Pharisees: all were amazed, astonished, in awe and afraid. And thirty years away from the events that was Jesus' life, Luke still finds himself amazed as well." –Michael Card, musician and author[2]

Who is astonished by Jesus in Luke 2:18, 2:47, and 2:48?

NOTABLE:

The Greek word *thaumazo* is used more than 40 times in the New Testament. Translated as to wonder, marvel, admire, flatter, astonish, amaze, *thaumazo* is the most common of all the Greek words that translate amaze. *Existemi* is used 17 times; *ekplesso* is used 13 times; *ekstasis* is used seven times; and *thambeo* is used four times. Throughout the Gospels, these five words almost always describe the attitudes of those listening to Jesus or witnessing His miracles.

As Jesus grows older and enters into His earthly ministry, those who hear His teaching are often spellbound and marvel at His words.

Why are listeners so amazed by Jesus in Luke 4:22, 4:32, and 4:36?

Jesus' miracles leave His followers amazed throughout Luke's Gospel. When the disciples are first instructed to throw their nets into deep water after a long night, they're astonished by the haul of fish they bring in (Luke 5:9). When Jesus heals a paralyzed man, they're filled with awe at the remarkable things they've seen (Luke 5:26).

A widow is astonished when Jesus gives her only son's life back (Luke 7:16), and everyone is amazed when a demon possessed boy is set free (Luke 9:43). On another occasion, a man is freed from a demon that rendered him mute, leaving the crowd marveling (Luke 11:14). And in the presence of some of the most brilliant teachers of the law, Jesus gives answers that leave even His accusers astonished (Luke 20:26).

The writing of Luke's Gospel challenges us that we are meant to live wide-eyed to the wonder of the amazing, mysterious, remarkable Person of Jesus Christ.

One last detail worth noting about this Gospel: Throughout the entire book, there's only one person who amazed Jesus.

Do you know who accomplished this feat? (Hint: Luke 7:1-9.)

The person wasn't a disciple or religious leader. Rather, he was a Roman centurion, an unlikely candidate to leave anyone astonished. Technically, the man doesn't give or do anything for Jesus, but the Son of God stands in amazement of this man.

Why is this man in Luke 7:1-9 such a source of amazement to the Son of God?

In all the Gospels, one consistent theme amazes Jesus.

Do you know what theme? (Hint: Mark 6:6.)

Think about this for a moment. The only things that cause Jesus to marvel are belief and unbelief or faith and lack of faith. This strikes me because God knows everything, yet He is still awed by our belief and faith or unbelief and lack of faith.

Would you rather live life like the Roman centurion or like the people in Nazareth described in Mark 6:6?

I don't know about you, but I want to live in such a way that I leave Jesus marveling, astonished, and wonderstruck—much like the Roman centurion.

Some of the wonders God wants to reveal are going to require us to believe in Him in greater measure and to make larger strides by faith. But make no mistake: Jesus will be cheering for us every step of the way.

Are you willing to make the journey?

If so, you're not going to want to miss the next lesson. The wonder of God's presence awaits.

CLOSING PRAYER: Spend some time asking God to give you a fresh sense of amazement of His faithfulness and presence in your life. Ask God to soften your heart to any areas where you've grown hard or disbelieving and give you the ability to trust Him wholeheartedly.

NOTABLE:

After witnessing Jesus heal a paralyzed man, Luke describes the people as being amazed in Luke 5:26. The word *amazed* is the Greek word *ekstasis*, which describes someone who is displaced out of a normal state of being or thinking. English derives the word *ecstasy* from this word. Usually, a person deemed insane or demon possessed is experiencing *ekstasis*, but the word also describes someone who witnesses something that is out of this world—a blended form of fear and wonderment. In the same verse, Luke describes the people as filled with awe. In the Greek, the people are filled with *phobos*, which literally translates fear or respect. The people are so displaced by what they saw, they are fearful. But they tell others what they've seen has left them wonderstruck.

THE WONDER OF GOD'S PRESENCE

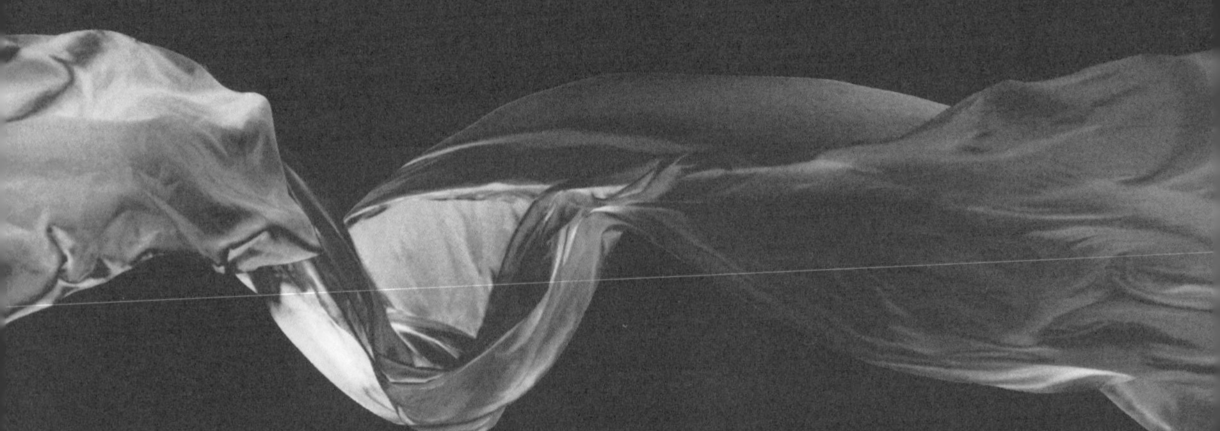

SESSION TWO

GROUP GETTING STARTED: (10-15 minutes)

SESSION TWO:
THE WONDER OF GOD'S PRESENCE

HOMEWORK GROUP DISCUSSION

1 One of the first activities you were asked to do in Day One's homework was to make daily entries into the Wonderstruck Journal on page 163. Share with the group three moments in which you've encountered the wonder of God and His handiwork this week.

2 Reflecting on all you've been reading and studying in *Wonderstruck*, how is praying for and living awake to wonder affecting your attitude and perspective on life and God?

3 In the homework from Day Two, you were asked what things prevent you from living with the expectation that God wants to do awesome work in, through, and around you. What did you list?

4 On Day Two, Margaret shares her struggles when she encounters a woman in need outside a grocery store. When have you found yourself in a similar situation? What stops you from taking bigger risks in your walk with God?

5 The final day of homework highlighted the sense of amazement that fills the Gospel of Luke. What were the two things that leave Jesus wonderstruck? (Hint: Luke 7:1-9 and Mark 6:6.) How does knowing what awes God affect the way that you want to live your life?

EXPERIENTIAL ACTIVITY: THE SWEETNESS OF GOD'S PRESENCE

WHAT YOU'LL NEED:

- A 3x5 card for each person
- A packet of markers

1 Hand a 3x5 card and marker to each participant.

2 Ask participants to write a verse from the Bible that has been particularly meaningful to them throughout their lives or in this season of life.

3 Then invite each participant to share what is written on their cards.

4 Discuss the following questions:

What circumstances were happening in your life when this passage first became meaningful to you?

How does this passage remind you of the faithfulness of God's presence in your life?

PLAY THE SESSION TWO VIDEO: [23:00]

NOTES

VIDEO DISCUSSION

1 Invite a participant to read Psalm 113 aloud. When in your life are you more tempted to focus on the *why*, *what*, *when*, and *how* (circumstances), rather than the *Who* (God's presence)?

2 When in your challenging times of life have you experienced God's presence?

3 What current situation in your life is causing you to focus more on the *why* (circumstances) than the *Who* (God's presence)?

4 How does focusing on the *Who* (God's presence) above all else tend to right size or prioritize things in your life?

CLOSING PRAYER

As you close in prayer ask that:

- each person's heart, mind, and life awaken to a greater sense of God's wonder
- God give each participant a deeper sense of His presence in their lives
- the Holy Spirit orchestrates a personal, private moment over the upcoming week when participants are reminded that the answers they seek are found in the *Who.*

DAY ONE

LIFE UNRAVELS SOMETIMES

THIS WEEK:

If you are following along in the trade book, read chapters ".002: Shock and Awe," and ".003: Alpenglow Evenings."

HAVE YOU EXPERIENCED one of those seasons of life where blow after blow, you couldn't win? Everything seems to be going wrong and the stress of it all weighs heavily on your shoulders. Recently, I endured a season where all I wanted to do was scream "Uncle!" at the top of my lungs.

Which of the following is more challenging to you? Mark your answer on the continuum below.

A single blow in life is more challenging for me to handle.	A series of smaller blows is more challenging for me to handle.

Why did you choose this response?

BONUS ACTIVITY:

Spend time committing Psalm 19:1 to memory this week. You'll find a flash card available on page 177.

For me, the series of smaller blows is far more difficult. A catastrophic moment of loss or pain is never pleasant, but when it's only one—I find I can migrate through the grieving process more steadily. When a series of smaller events hit, I feel like as soon as I start making progress in grieving one loss, I return to the beginning again until it begins to feel like life has completely unraveled.

Have you experienced a catastrophic life event? Mark the ones you've experienced personally:

- ☐ **the death of a loved one**
- ☐ **the diagnosis of an incurable disease**
- ☐ **the loss of a job**
- ☐ **infertility**
- ☐ **a natural disaster**
- ☐ **chronic illness**
- ☐ **irreparable personal injury**
- ☐ **divorce—either your parents' marriage or yours**
- ☐ **change in living or work situation**
- ☐ **giving up an addiction**

How many of these have you experienced in the last year?

Catastrophic events as well as less cataclysmic events, which can create upheaval, require us to go through a grieving process. Sometimes the loss we feel can happen when a close friend moves across the country or when a pet dies. We can try to tell ourselves a thousand times over that we shouldn't be feeling what we're feeling, but this doesn't negate the emotions or thoughts. We must come to terms with the loss or pain in order to move forward in life and with God.

If you're not familiar with the Five Stages of Grief, they include:

1 **SHOCK AND DENIAL.** This includes a sense of numbness or denying the reality of the loss at some level. Common phrases used during this stage include, "I can't believe this is happening to me" and "I'm fine."

2 **PAIN AND ANGER.** Once the shock wears off, it's often replaced by pain and a buildup of anger that needs a healthy release. Common phrases used during this stage include, "Why me?" and "Why did God allow this?" and "Who is to blame for this?"

3 **BARGAINING.** This stage often includes bargaining that "If I promise to fill-in-the-blank, then ..." with ourselves, God, and others.

4 **DEPRESSION.** Though it's tempting to believe the grieving is over, sadness eventually sets in. The temptation for some is isolation that allows one to slide into a deeper depression or even despair. Common phrases include, "I don't have the energy to do anything," and "We're all going to die soon anyway."

5 **ACCEPTANCE.** This is the final stage of grief that allows one to accept the reality of the situation and find a way to move forward. Common phrases include, "It's going to be OK" and "I know I can't fight this anymore, but with God I can face it."

Which of the stages of grief listed above have you experienced?

BONUS ACTIVITY:

A helpful tool I've used to gauge the amount of tension in my life is the Holmes and Rahe Stress Scale, which looks at how events in the past year create health-impacting stress. I highly recommend taking this test at least once each year. Take the test on your own or as a group and discuss. You can find a free version online by Googling it.

NOTABLE:

The breakdown of the Stages of Grief varies widely and can include as few as three or more than ten, but the basic outline of those stages are highlighted in the five stages listed.

With which of the stages of grief do you tend to struggle or become stuck on most?

What comfort does Psalm 46:1 provide in these moments?

QUOTABLE:

In the most opaque circumstances of life, even when He feels a million miles away, the knowledge of the presence of God allows us to find joy when everything else says we should be crying.

At the moment I'm writing this session, one of my extended family members is dying of cancer. The family is flying in to say their goodbyes. Anyone who knows someone who has battled cancer knows it's a vicious, ugly disease. Each family member and friend involved is in a different stage of their grieving process. It's messy, painful, and heartbreaking. As I reflect on the stages above, I think I'm somewhere between stage 2 and 3. I'm both mad at the disease and bargaining with God. Yet I know that God wants to reveal Himself even in the midst of this painful journey—not just to me but to every family member and friend.

As followers of Jesus, I believe God wants to meet us at every stage and every moment of the grieving process. God wants to reveal that He is with us. He hears us. He loves us. And He has not left us. At times, God wants to speak into our grieving and sense of loss and reorient us to one of the greatest wonders of all: His presence.

In our greatest moments of pain, loss, and heartache, God wants to anchor us to the reality of His imminence. We do not serve a God who is far off, but One who is near and draws near to those shattered by life. God isn't only with us in those moments, but all the moments. He longs to reveal His presence and purpose in that which we do not understand.

God doesn't ask us to deny our grief, but to seek Him in the midst of grief. The invitation to awaken to the wonder of God's presence remains—even in the affliction, even in the loss, even in the pain. As we begin to seek Him, our focus shifts from downward to upward, from inward to outward.

NOTABLE:

Why questions are those that surround the circumstance. *Who* questions draw our attention and focus back to God.

Instead of focusing on the *Why's* of our life circumstances, God calls our attention back to Him and reminds us of the *Who* that controls everything.

Do you tend to focus on the *Why* or the *Who* in the midst of life's challenges?

What does it look like for you to pursue God in the moments when life unravels?

No matter where you are in life or what you're facing, may God open your eyes to the Great *Who* in your midst.

CLOSING PRAYER: Spend some time asking God to reveal any areas in your life where your focus is still on the *Why* rather than the *Who*. Ask God to reveal His presence and speak to you in a way that leaves you wonderstruck.

DAY TWO

GOD WELCOMES THE WHY

SOMETIMES I'M TEMPTED to hold back my toughest questions from God. I convince myself that if I don't say things aloud then maybe they won't be true or maybe they'll go away. Or I tell myself that if I really told God what I truly thought, what I was really wrestling with, somehow He couldn't take it. None of these beliefs are true or healthy.

We serve a God who wants us to give ourselves—our whole selves—to Him. This includes our doubts and determinations, our fear and frustrations, our aches and aspirations, our hollow as well as hallowed spaces. One of the most treasured places in the Bible where this wild honesty with God appears is in the Psalms.

The Book of Psalms is divided into five books, each ending with a doxology or concluding word of praise. Psalm 1 offers the introduction, and Psalm 150 is the concluding doxology for the entire collection.

Psalms contains an eclectic collection of 150 songs, prayers, and poems. Some were written by David, but most were penned by a band of anonymous poets and musicians. Some psalms were used in worship services as a type of liturgy (Psalms 2 and 50), others expressed thanksgiving or praise (Psalms 18; 107; 138), while still others celebrated the saving actions of God from the past and His promises and faithfulness (Psalm 131).

NOTABLE:

Psalm 55 expresses a plea for deliverance from one's enemies, and verses 12-14 and 20-21 uniquely point toward the betrayal of a close friend.

But some of the most vivid and starkly honest psalms are the laments. In a lament, emotions run lava hot in all directions. Feelings of being distraught, in anguish, fear, and in pain all appear in less than three breaths.

What emotions does the Psalmist express in Psalm 55:2-5?

Which of the emotions have you felt or experienced?

Which of the emotions have you freely expressed to God?

Which have you tried to hold back at one time or another? Why?

Among the laments, questions abound. Those who lament poke and prod God with timeless open-ended questions of *Why?*, *Where are You?*, and *Why have You forsaken me?*

What questions do the following verses ask of God?

Psalm 10:1:

Psalm 22:1:

Psalm 42:3:

Circle the questions you have asked in your spiritual journey.

What other questions have you asked?

NOTABLE:

Psalm 22 prophetically reflects Jesus' suffering and death on the cross, but don't miss the original meaning for the psalmist. The psalmist writes out of desperation after feeling forsaken by God. Jesus spoke the words of Psalm 22:1 on the cross in Aramaic as recorded in Matthew 27:46 and Mark 15:34.

If you could ask God one burning question right now, what would you ask?

The shocking statements and tough questions found in lament psalms aren't intended to sanctify our vindictive thoughts or bad behavior. Rather they invite us to come honestly as we are into the presence of God and experience transformation. In laying hold of what we really feel, we can seek healing and redemption.

That's the key element to a good lament. While the entry may express a wide range of emotions to God, a subtle transformation often takes place in the psalmist's heart: beginning at the low point of suffering but ending with renewed faith in God. The psalmist reorients his life Godward through lamenting. Starting with one perspective, the psalmist ends with a completely different outlook.

The crux of a lament isn't about letting everything hang out with God or embracing a good cry, but embracing the work of reflection and soul-searching, a kind of spiritual self-examination. The heart shift that takes place during a lament isn't an apple-pie-in-the-sky kind of hopefulness, but a deep conviction in the One who provides deliverance.

NOTABLE:

Personal and corporate laments can be determined by the point of view used—either first person (personal lament) or third person (corporate lament).

Unlike personal laments such as Psalms 10, 22, and 42, Psalm 74 is a corporate lament of the Israelites crying out during the Babylonian exile—a period of 70 years when the Israelites were forced out of their land by the Babylonians.

How does the focus of the Psalmist change throughout Psalm 74?

How do you think writing a lament like Psalm 74 could strengthen your faith and connection with God?

By creating my own laments, I discovered a safe place and approach to release emotions and ask tough questions of God.

Now such writing doesn't come without a few guidelines. Though the Psalms have been described as a kind of First Amendment of the faithful[3], we still must exercise our freedom in a way that brings healing rather than further heartache to ourselves, others, and God. While creativity and colorful imagery are welcomed, the lament isn't a place to curse anyone or make "I will never" vows that only deepen the pain. A healthy lament is designed to provide space to feel and release emotions over time, ask the hard questions, and seek to develop a glimmer of praise, even if only in kernel form, of the goodness of God. A good lament will always move us from the *Why* to the *Who*.

Over the years I've written laments, I've found them to be a source of healing. Something about the process of asking the tough questions—including *Why*—and being honest about the hurts have opened the door to further healing from God in my life.

Maybe you're facing a loss or difficult situation right now, or maybe you have something in the past and you haven't taken the time to get it out with God. Maybe you're afraid of the emotions you'll feel if you really allow yourself to feel. Maybe you're scared that if you're really honest with God that somehow He'll pull back from you.

+ BONUS ACTIVITY:

Don't forget to add to your Wonderstruck Journal today.

NOTABLE:

Lament psalms often contain the following elements: an invocation for God, a complaint of distress, a petition for intervention or vengeance, a confession of sin or proclamation of innocence, a vow to praise God for deliverance, an expression of trust in God, and a final praise.

WRITING YOUR OWN LAMENT

I'd like to challenge you to be brave and let out whatever you're feeling in the form of a lament. Write your own lament below. Consider including the biggest burning question you're facing right now, as well as the emotions you're feeling, and cry out to God in the midst of remembering that He is the source of hope and healing. If you're stumped, turn to Psalm 13 as an example of a lament to guide you.

Being honest with God is nothing new. I have cried, yelled, shouted, and screamed at God countless times before. More recently, I told God that I think He has terrible theology. I think He laughed at least twice. But something about a lament invites us to rediscover God's goodness and never-ending love even in the darkest of times. Lament gives us the opportunity to turn on a dime in our relationship with God and others. We're invited to flip flop from loss to trust, from pain to praise—wholly reorienting our lives toward God.

Why is that so important?

Because we can't have an intimate relationship with others with whom we do not speak honestly.

By showing our true selves to God—questions, emotions, and all—we discover God's love in greater measure. God listens to our stinging words, embraces our frail hearts, and meets us where we are.

My hope and prayer is that this will be just one of many laments you'll take time to write to God and in the process discover His healing touch and presence in greater measure.

CLOSING PRAYER: Spend some time reading your lament aloud to God as a prayer. Offer each word deliberately and intentionally. Ask God to meet you in the midst of the lament as He did for so many psalmists before you.

DAY THREE

GOD MEETS US IN THE WHO

IN YESTERDAY'S LESSON, we looked at the idea that God can handle our toughest questions. No matter what we're going through, God wants to meet us there. But in His love, God doesn't leave us there. Though God welcomes all of our questions—even the countless *Why* questions—He invites us to reorient our focus on the *Who*.

This is demonstrated in the life of Job—a good man who is overwhelmed by trouble, loss, and a most unfortunate series of events. From the beginning of the Book of Job, arguably the oldest book in the Bible, Job is portrayed as upright and pleasing to God.

In the space below, make a list of the details from Job 1:1-5 signifying that Job was devout and blessed by God.

You may have noted the adjectives used to describe Job. Or you may have noted the number of Job's children—seven sons and three daughters—both of those numbers are representative of wholeness or completeness. You may have noticed his success as a businessman or how, even at the thought that his children could have sinned, Job offers sacrifices on their behalf. Yet despite his faithfulness, calamity is unleashed in Job's life.

How do you tend to respond when you see bad things happen to other people? Place a check mark by your most common responses below.

- ☐ **pulling your hair out in frustration**
- ☐ **dropping your jaw in disbelief**
- ☐ **bringing on the waterworks**
- ☐ **wrestling with God**
- ☐ **other:**

QUOTABLE:

"The book of Job is ... the story of one man, his loss, his search and his discovery. This search takes place entirely within the household of faith. All the characters, the three friends and Elihu as much as Job himself, are fully committed to belief in one supreme God who is unquestionably just in all his acts. Solutions which lie outside such biblical revelation are not even considered in the book of Job." –Francis Anderson, biblical scholar[4]

How do you respond when bad things happen in your life? Place a check mark by your most common responses below.

- ☐ **pulling your hair out in frustration**
- ☐ **dropping your jaw in disbelief**
- ☐ **bringing on the waterworks**
- ☐ **wrestling with God**
- ☐ **other:**

In a series of devastating blows, Job loses his children, livestock, wealth, and health. Throughout the Book of Job, we begin to look at just how bad life has become for this upright man.

Read the following passages and summarize what the Scripture records about Job's misery:

Job 2:7:

Job 7:4-5:

Job 7:14:

Job 7:16:

Job 16:16:

Job 19:17-20:

Job 30:28-30:

NOTABLE:

Job 19 records Job calling out for a redeemer—an idea in the Old Testament of one who is an advocate, an avenger of blood, or a liberator from sin. Job cries out for God, his Redeemer who will remain even after Job's death.

QUOTABLE:

"God doesn't reveal his grand design (to Job). He reveals Himself. He doesn't show why things are as they are. He shows his face. And Job says, 'I had heard of thee by the hearing of the ear, but now my eyes see thee.' Even covered with sores and ashes, he looks oddly like a man who has asked for a crust and been given the whole loaf." –Frederick Buechner, biblical scholar[5]

These descriptions portray a man who is experiencing extreme pain and disfigurement. Draw a picture of what you imagine Job looks like according to the passages you read.

NOTABLE:

The Book of Job brings up the false belief of retribution theology, which suggests if one is suffering, one must have sinned. Job's friends, Eliphaz, Bildad, Zophar, and Elihu all believe Job is getting what he deserves. Both Job and God have an issue with this belief.

Despite this portrait of suffering, Job refuses to curse God. Nowhere does Job bemoan the losses described in the first chapter of the book. Job's concern isn't his wealth or health, but rather his relationship with God. Despite all the physical torment, the real torment for Job is that he feels like he has lost God. Job's concerns circle around the question of *Why*. He wants to know what he may have done that has made God seem so distant. In response, all Job hears is silence.

When is a time you asked God to speak and been met with silence? What do you find most challenging about the silence of God?

When in your life have you felt a million miles from God? What tough questions did you ask God during that time?

Job's well-meaning friends offer little comfort in the midst of Job's suffering. The One who Job needs to hear from most is God. For me, this is when Job's character truly shines. Even in the midst of the silence, Job keeps talking. Job keeps asking God to speak. Job refuses to quit pursuing God.

Until Job 38, God seems to stand back quietly admiring Job's character and response. When God finally breaks the silence, He takes Job's breath away. God approaches Job in the form of a whirlwind and asks Job to stand up (Job 38:2-3). God doesn't want to crush Job with the awareness of his smallness, but to expose Job to His limitless power, tender care, and constant presence in the world.

In the space below, record all of the *Who* questions God asks Job in Job 38–41. Place a star by the *Who* questions that strengthen your resolve to place your faith in God.

Reflecting on God's speech, on the continuum below mark whether you focus more on the *Why* (circumstances) or the *Who* (God's presence) when facing difficult times:

Why (circumstances) —————————— *Who* (God's presence)

In the wake of God's powerful, poetic soliloquy, Job finds himself undone. Job confesses the power and sovereignty of God and finds his knowledge of God has expanded in profound ways. Job's perspective shifts as he acknowledges that in God everything is simply too wonderful for him to understand (Job 42:3). This is the response of a joyful and liberated man—a man who has encountered the presence of God.

QUOTABLE:

"You asked, 'Who is this that obscures my plans without knowledge?' Surely I spoke of things I did not understand, things too wonderful for me to know." –Job 42:3

What difference would focusing on the *Who* instead of the *Why* make in the situations you're facing right now?

In whatever situation you find yourself right now, I pray that through the Holy Spirit you'll begin experiencing a shift in your perspective from the *Why* to the *Who*. And that even in the silence you'll be courageous and keep talking to God. A day is coming when God will break the silence and you'll have knowledge of God that will leave you with a renewed sense of wonder.

CLOSING PRAYER: Spend some time thanking God for the work He has yet to do in your life. Thank God simply for who He is.

DAY FOUR

THE GREAT GIFT OF I AM

NOTABLE:

In Exodus 33, we see Moses talking with God on behalf of the Israelites. God plans on destroying Israel for their disobedience, but Moses seems to influence the outcome by engaging with God. One of the biggest takeaways of this passage is seeing the contrast between selfish Moses in Exodus 3 and brave intercessor Moses in Exodus 33.

ONE OF THE GREATEST WONDERS OF GOD is His presence. Over the years, I've discovered that even a brief moment in the presence of God can change everything—my perspective, attitude, and reaction. Being aware of and experiencing God's presence reminds me of my dependence on God. He is the source of everything—joy, provision, protection, love, grace, mercy, hope, and so much more.

Yet despite the sweetness and delight of God's presence, I'm amazed at how often I forget to take time to be with God. Though I may spend time in the morning studying the Scripture or praying, I'll say amen and run off toward projects and deadlines. In the process I hush that still silent voice that beckons me to linger—to sit in the silence and simply be with God.

How did Joshua's response to God's presence differ from the people's response in Exodus 33:9-11?

When in your life have you sensed God's Spirit beckoning you to linger with God?

How did you respond?

NOTABLE:

A sacred echo describes the repetitive nature of God's voice—marking those moments when God speaks again and again in our lives.

When I skip such moments, I tend to be less aware of God throughout my day. I miss divine moments when God wants to meet me or reveal a new facet of His character. I find myself less sensitive to the nudges of the Holy Spirit, the sacred echoes that call me to give, serve, or say the kind word.

We are created for a relationship with God, and that means we're meant to experience God's presence. We need God's presence and the awareness of His nearness if we're going to grow into the fullness of all God intends. Apart from His presence, we can begin to convince ourselves that somehow God is distant; somehow we can handle things on our own.

Maybe this is one reason God keeps echoing throughout the Scripture, "I am with you! I am with you! I am with you!"

In the last week, when have you been reminded of God's presence in your life?

How did the awareness of God's presence affect your attitude, perspective, or response to others in the moment?

QUOTABLE:

"'I am the Alpha and the Omega,' says the Lord God, 'who is, and who was, and who is to come, the Almighty.'" –Revelation 1:8

One of the ways God identifies Himself is using the first and last letter of the Greek alphabet. In Revelation 1:8; 21:6; and 22:13, Jesus is revealed as the Alpha and the Omega. One of the books of the Bible most riddled with mystery introduces this title in its first and last chapter—as if bookends to declare, "I'm holding it all together!"

Years ago, I read that when the Jewish people used this title for God in their language they call Him the *"Aleph"* and the *"Tav"*—the first and last letter of the Hebrew alphabet. But they also like to refer to Him as the *"Mem"* which is the middlemost letter of the Hebrew alphabet. Why? Because they recognize God doesn't only go before them or after them, but He is with them every step of the way.

How have you discovered God as the "Mem" in your spiritual journey?

NOTABLE:

The title "the Alpha and the Omega" should be read as the One who is, and who was, and who is to come—indicating that God is eternal. Often Greeks used letters to represent various gods. As John writes Revelation, he uses this title to describe God as the God of all gods.

One story depicting the faithfulness of God and His presence is in the Book of Exodus. God's people, the Israelites, are under the wicked rule of the Pharaoh at the time, but their suffering does not escape His notice. In love, God calls an unsuspecting man, Moses, to demand the Israelites' freedom. Moses responds with a trunk full of self-doubt and a laundry list of questions. As a pragmatist, Moses asks, "If I go to the people and claim that the God of your fathers has sent me to you and they ask me for Your name, what should I tell them?"

That's when God reveals Himself in the most unexpected way.

What does the name God gives Moses in Exodus 3:13-15 reveal to you about the character of God?

NOTABLE:

The name "I AM" that God reveals to Moses is the tetragrammaton, written *YHWH*, the holy name of God. Jews would refrain from pronouncing the sacred Name. They replaced *YHWH* with *Adonai*, meaning *Lord*. Somewhere along the way some of the vowels from *Adonai* combined with the consonants in *YHWH* creating the word *Jehovah*.

God could have offered Moses many different names, but God chooses to reveal Himself as "I AM" or what some translate as "I Am Who I Am." This is a powerful insight into the character of God. By revealing His name to the people, God demonstrates that He wants relationship with them—to be known by them. The name "I AM" also reveals facets of the character of God. "I AM" suggests that God's presence has no beginning or end. God is ever present. The name also hints at the mysterious nature of God. Though God longs to be known, there are aspects of God we'll never be able to wrap our minds around. The divine name also shows God's faithfulness.

QUOTABLE:

"'Very truly I tell you,' Jesus answered, 'before Abraham was born, I am!'" –John 8:58

Years ago, I had a friend who was going through a really tough time. She had been crying out to God to speak, to move, to do something miraculous in the midst of the impossible situation she faced. One day as she prayed, she sensed God say two words: I AM.

Those tiny words said everything she needed to hear at that moment. The wonder of God's presence was alive in her heart, mind, and spirit. She knew that even though she didn't have the answers, even though nothing changed from the outside, something shifted deep within her. Her struggle did not go unnoticed. God was with her.

When in your life have you experienced God as I AM? Record at least one of your answers in your Wonderstruck Journal on page 164.

In what situations do you need to experience God as I AM right now? Make a list in the space below. Then prayerfully ask God to reveal Himself and His presence in each one.

NOTABLE:

Throughout the Gospel of John, Jesus proclaims seven I AM statements, which point back to Exodus 3:13-15 and establish that Jesus is indeed the Son of God.

What comfort do you find in knowing God as "I AM" in the midst of the situations and challenges you're currently facing?

I pray that God will reveal Himself in the middle of whatever situation, challenge, or hardship you're facing right now. May you know the great I AM like never before.

CLOSING PRAYER: Spend some time asking God to reveal Himself as I AM in specific situations where you haven't experienced Him before. Ask for the wonder of God's presence to become a source of delight and joy that beams through you.

DAY FIVE

THE WONDER OF CREATION

SOMETIMES I LET MY MIND WANDER to all of the ways God could have answered Job in the midst of his pain, loss, and hardship.

God could have worn an academic cap and explained in theological terms what was happening to Job.

God could have secured a helmet and described in sporting terms what was happening to Job.

God could have tugged a hoodie over His head and chosen to hide as He explained in mysterious terms what was happening to Job.

Instead, God wears a safari hat and takes Job on an unforgettable and wild tour of creation. God points to nature to instruct Job. God peppers Job with questions such as, "Who cuts a channel for the torrents of rain, and a path for the thunderstorm?" (Job 38:25) and "Who has the wisdom to count the clouds?" (v. 37).

To which only one appropriate answer exists.

QUOTABLE:

"He spreads the snow like wool and scatters the frost like ashes. He hurls down his hail like pebbles. Who can withstand his icy blast?" –Psalm 147:16-17

Through God's breathtaking speech, Job is invited by the designer of the cosmos to reflect on the constellations of the night's sky (Job 38:31-33) and the cumulus clouds of a summer's day (vv. 34-38) through different lenses. More than a tour from the zookeeper or botanist, the Creator of all embarks alongside Job on a sacred safari that includes donkeys (39:5), wild ox (v. 9), ostriches (v. 13), hawks (v. 26), eagles (v. 27) and much, much more. After listening to God, Job simply can't see any creature—whether a lion (38:39-40) or a mountain goat (39:1)—the same way again.

And neither should we.

Now let me be very clear: Creation is never to be worshiped, but creation beckons us to seek God and worship the Creator. Throughout creation, we have countless opportunities to catch glimpses of God's handiwork and admire different facets of His character that will leave us wonderstruck.

What aspects of creation in Romans 1:20 are used to reveal the invisible qualities of God?

What does Proverbs 3:19-20 reveal about God's wisdom?

What aspects of creation in Psalm 36:5-6 are used to reveal the love, faithfulness, righteousness, and justice of God?

When you spend time outside, do you expect to experience the promise of Psalm 19:1? Why or why not?

BONUS ACTIVITY:

One of my favorite websites for embarking on a Bible safari is *www.creationsafaris.com/csbibref.htm*, which provides hundreds of references to creation throughout the Bible. The list is breathtaking in and of itself.

The signs and symbols of redemption, the message of God's love, are woven throughout the natural world from the foundation of the world. On the second day of creation, God separated the water from the firmament, and even now the splash of an icy river whispers of the sacrament of baptism and invites us to reflect on the crucial role water plays throughout the Bible. Such moments are meant to leave us wonderstruck.

When was the last time you encountered something in nature that nurtured your desire or appreciation for God?

NOTABLE:

Did you know the rings of Saturn are braided? What kind of God takes time to braid the rings of a planet?

The appearance of land and vegetation on the third day of creation foreshadows the plants, vines, and trees that appear in countless stories in the Scripture. Without wheat or grapes we could not celebrate the Lord's Supper. During early evening walks through the neighborhood park, we have the opportunity to have our hearts drawn Godward with every leaf and wildflower.

The pattern continues throughout the Genesis story—animals and elements appear that will reappear throughout the great big story of God. We shouldn't be surprised when Jesus encourages the disciples not to worry, He points to the lilies of the field (Matthew 6:28) and the precious life of a sparrow (Matthew 10:29).

On the chart below, fill in what Bible stories or sacred observations are possible because of what God created on the first six days of creation: For example, the story of Jonah is possible because of days three and five, and the magi following the star at Christ's birth is possible because of day four.

NOTABLE:

On an unsuspecting morning I awake before my alarm and slip out of bed. I look out and see the golden glow of sunrise harkening the announcement that God's mercies are renewed each morning (Lamentations 3:22-23).

DAY OF CREATION:	BIBLE PASSAGES/STORIES:
DAY ONE: heavens and earth, light and darkness	
DAY TWO: atmosphere or sky	
DAY THREE: dry land, sea, vegetation	
DAY FOUR: sun, moon, stars	
DAY FIVE: creatures in water, birds in air	
DAY SIX: land animals and people	

God's nature is revealed in nature. I've experienced this in my life on countless days and nights leaving me awestruck by God's presence. Looking out at breathtaking views, I can't help but wonder, *Who am I that God, the One who created all things, would desire a relationship with me?*

While hiking a steep mountain, I'm reminded of the importance of perseverance and tenacity in my spiritual journey and rediscover at the summit that nothing is impossible with God. Standing on a white sand beach, I look across the ocean and glimpse the vastness and power of God. In an instant my world becomes right sized.

Looking up into a dark starry night, I can't help but reflect on the promise given to Abraham concerning his descendants and catch a glimmer of God's faithfulness. In the stillness, I thank God for such beauty. Such sights are nature's way of reminding us to look up, down, and all around for God and prayerfully consider the work He wants to do in our lives.

Describe a time when you were out in nature and discovered more about God's nature.

BONUS ACTIVITY:

A fabulous website for reflecting on the size of the universe is *www.htwins.net/scale2/*. Check it out!

When you step outside into creation, do you expect to encounter the Creator? Why or why not?

What can you do right now to develop rhythms in your life that foster spiritual vitality and a greater awareness of God through creation?

In the next lesson, we're going to dive into one of the wonders of God that we all need to experience: rest. You won't want to miss the next video session!

CLOSING PRAYER: Spend some time outside or looking out a window admiring God's creation—a patch of grass, a shaft of sunlight overhead, a shade of blue unimaginable. Thank God for the attributes of His character you see reflected through creation. And if you catch a glimpse of God's wonder, don't forget to record what you see in the Wonderstruck Journal.

THE WONDER OF REST

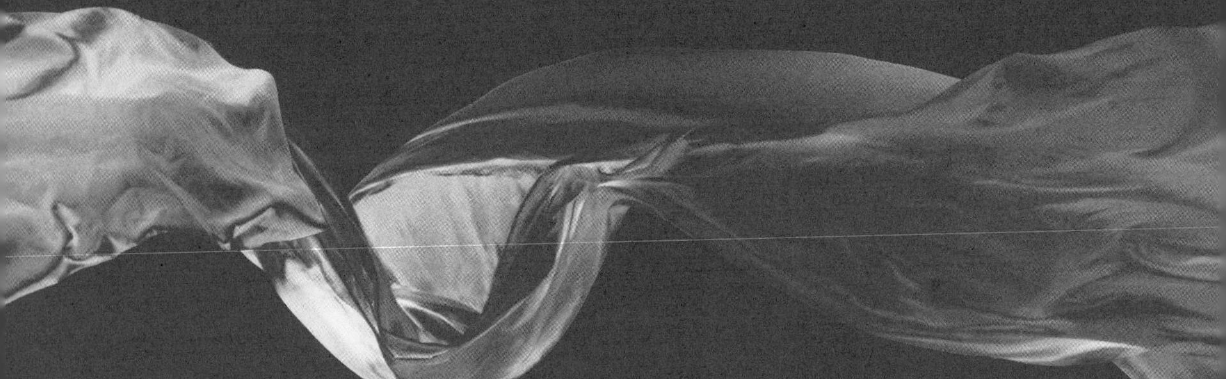

SESSION THREE

GROUP GETTING STARTED: (10-15 minutes)

SESSION THREE: THE WONDER OF REST

HOMEWORK GROUP DISCUSSION

1 From their Wonderstruck Journal on page 163, ask participants to share three moments in which they encountered the wonder of God and His handiwork this week.

2 In the first day's homework, you were asked to consider areas where God is challenging you to shift from asking *Why* to asking *Who*. In what area of your life did you sense the Holy Spirit saying it's time to start asking *Who* in this situation? What did God reveal as you began asking *Who*?

3 What did you learn or discover through writing your own psalm of lament as part of the homework for Day Two?

4 As part of the homework for Day Three, you were asked to look up Scripture about Job and then draw a picture of him. Share your picture with the group. As you studied Job's story throughout the homework, what most stood out to you about his life and journey?

5 Share your responses to the following questions, which were part of Day Four's homework: In the last week, when have you been reminded of God's presence in your life? How did the awareness of God's presence affect your attitude, perspective, or response to others in the moment?

6 Reflecting on the final day's homework, what have you done in the past week to nurture more of the wonder of God's creation in your life?

EXPERIENTIAL ACTIVITY: A 5-MINUTE REST

WHAT YOU'LL NEED:

- A place in or near the room where you gather that has two couches or chairs with ottomans for people to stretch out
- A clock

1 Ask for two volunteers who are willing to try to fall asleep in the next five minutes. These two volunteers can lie down or find a cozy chair to rest in.

2 Set the clock for five minutes.

3 While the volunteers are trying to rest, discuss among the group the rituals they use each night to prepare for bed.

4 When the five minutes is up, ask within earshot of the volunteers, "Will those who are still awake please raise their hands?"

5 Discuss the following questions:

What was the easiest and hardest part of falling asleep for each volunteer?

What prevents you from slowing down, resting more, and savoring the gift of life that God has entrusted you with?[6]

PLAY THE SESSION THREE VIDEO: [21:15]

NOTES

VIDEO DISCUSSION

1 What are the top three things preventing you from entering that place in space and time God has for you to rest and encounter Him?

2 Describe the last time you entered that place in space and time to be "deposited into" by God. How did that moment of resting and receiving from Him reorient your perspective and attitude?

3 In what areas of your life are you prone to overcommit and overextend?

4 Read Hebrews 4:9-11. What healthy rhythms do you need to establish in your work, relationships, and daily schedule—including the Sabbath—to seize the life God has for you?

CLOSING PRAYER

As you close in prayer, ask:

- for each person's heart, mind, and life to awaken to a greater sense of the wonder of God
- for the determination to pursue physical and spiritual rest and rejuvenation
- the Holy Spirit to illuminate areas and opportunities in which each person needs to say no in order to say yes to all God has in store.

DAY ONE

REDISCOVERING REST

THIS WEEK:

If you are following along in the trade book, read chapter ".004: A Sanctuary in Time."

ALL TOO OFTEN I FIND myself burning the candle at both ends … and in the middle. A schedule crammed with deadlines to make, people to entertain, and places to be leaves little downtime.

When have you most recently found yourself burnt out?

How would you describe your physical, spiritual, and emotional state during that time?

I knew I needed someone to talk to who could help me identify the source of my exhaustion. A friend of mine mentioned a counseling center a few months earlier that had helped make a difference in her life. I decided to give the office a call.

Have you ever spoken to a Christian counselor about an issue you've been through in your past or are facing in your present?

BONUS ACTIVITY:

Spend time committing Matthew 11:28-30 to memory this week. You'll find a flash card on page 177.

If not, what's stopping you from making that connection?

If so, what difference did the Christian counselor make in your life?

How are you comforted by King Solomon's words in Proverbs 12:15?

QUOTABLE:

"The words of the reckless pierce like swords, but the tongue of the wise brings healing." –Proverbs 12:18

Sometimes to make healthy changes we need the support of others. We need people who will ask us the hard questions and offer a fresh perspective as well as practical solutions to the issues we're facing. This may mean turning to a professional counselor who can help us identify the unhealthy patterns in our life and their source in order to set a new healthier course. Or this may mean turning to friends who know us, love us, and can challenge us to become all we're created by God to be.

Who do you have to talk to when you're facing challenging circumstances or events?

QUOTABLE:

"Walk with the wise and become wise, for a companion of fools suffers harm." –Proverbs 13:20

What are you doing to nurture the relationships with the people you just listed?

One of the biggest insights the counselor helped me discover was that I never developed healthy boundaries telling me when to stop. This is only compounded by the fact that I love what I do. If life is a treadmill, then the counselor observed I'd been running at a level 10 with an incline of 10 since childhood.

The analogy explained why I felt tired on the inside. I could sleep 10 hours but still wake up exhausted. I lived in a world where small things loomed large while large things remained unnoticed. The hurly burly of life stood in the way of truly living.

As we discussed the word picture, my mind wandered to people with whom I'd been impatient because they couldn't keep up the pace. I recalled specific moments when my emotional response had been disproportionate to a situation. The pace of my life was making me increasingly un-Christlike.

On the continuum below, mark how a faster pace in your life affects you.

A faster pace makes me more Christlike. ——— A faster pace makes me less Christlike.

The Christian counselor I spent time with challenged me to reflect on the pace of my life. Below are a few of the questions I wrestled with. How would you respond to each one?

Number of hours you worked this week:

Number of hours you worked last week:

Number of hours you slept last night:

Number of hours you sleep on average:

Number of weeks since you took a vacation:

What set times have you built into your schedule for reflection and relaxation?

I don't know about you, but I didn't always like my answers. They exposed that I hadn't taken a vacation in more than four years, and I wasn't being intentional about setting apart time for rest.

Leif and I began setting a reasonable bedtime as well as a time to stop work. We recommitted to exercising on a regular basis, no matter how tired we felt. Over time, we found ourselves more well rested, engaged, and quick to laugh.

I began to discover the wonder of rest. When well rested, I'm more attuned to the presence of God and the leadings of the Holy Spirit. When my sleep bank is full, I'm more ready to see and respond to opportunities to serve, give, and encourage. When I embrace downtime, I'm more awake to the countless wonders of God all around—in relationships, divine encounters, and everyday life.

Do you feel like you're giving your best self to your relationships and work? Why or why not?

NOTABLE:

Rest asks us to wash our hands from the busyness of everyday life and find refreshment in the One who holds all things together.

What changes could you make in your daily schedule that would add even a few moments of much-needed downtime?

Will you commit to begin making those changes today?

I pray you won't miss this opportunity to reassess your schedule and become more intentional about experiencing the wonder of rest in your life.

CLOSING PRAYER: Spend some time reflecting on your personal schedule and ask God to highlight areas where He's asking you either to cut back or become more engaged. Prayerfully consider making changes regarding bedtimes, wake times, downtimes, and exercise that can help you live more awake and alive to the wonders of God.

DAY TWO

THE PAUSE AWAKENS US TO GOD

SLEEP DEPRIVATION TAKES A HEAVY TOLL on our minds and bodies. Scientists show that insufficient amounts of sleep affect the part of the brain that controls language, memory, sense of time, and our ability to plan. In addition, the body performs less efficiently and isn't able to recharge the immune system as well. But lack of sleep also affects our spiritual lives.

NOTABLE:

Loss of just one and a half hours of sleep can result in a 32% reduction in daytime alertness.[7]

When I'm physically tired, weary, or stressed, I'm less likely to live with an awareness of the Holy Spirit. Below I have listed some of the signs that show lack of rest is taking a toll in my life.

As you read, place a star next to any you've noticed recently in yours.

_ MY MORNING TIMES OF STUDY AND PRAYER BECOME MORE RUSHED.

_ I PASSED BY COUNTLESS PEOPLE WITHOUT REALLY SEEING THEM—OR THEIR NEEDS.

_ I RUSHED BY MOMENTS OF GRACE AND GOD'S GOODNESS UNAWARE. I HUSH THE HOLY SPIRIT'S NUDGES BY RESPONDING, "I DON'T HAVE TIME."

How does lack of rest make you dull to the things of God?

BONUS ACTIVITY:

You don't need to spend a fortune to get away. One of my favorite sites for finding somewhere to stay is *www.airbnb.com*. You can rent someone's apartment, condo, or even a spare bedroom anywhere in the world—and while you're gone, rent out your own.

Years ago someone asked me, "What's the biggest thing that causes you to sin?" I thought about the question for while. I considered the temptation to overeat at a fancy buffet, the advertisement of that sexy shirtless guy, the juiciness of gossip, the enticement of breaking the rules, the pride that so easily creeps into our hearts, and much more. Temptation takes so many different forms. But when I reflected on what causes me to sin the most, I had only one answer:

Lack of sleep.

That may sound silly at first, but when I don't get enough sleep, I'm more likely to stumble into any temptation before me. The resolve to stay strong, remain pure, or be courageous melts away. Without enough rest, I become increasingly impatient and unloving, more susceptible to fear, and easily angered.

What temptations are you more prone to give in to when you haven't gotten enough rest?

How does getting enough rest help you yield to righteousness as described in Romans 6:19?

QUOTABLE:

"No temptation has overtaken you except what is common to mankind. And God is faithful; he will not let you be tempted beyond what you can bear. But when you are tempted, he will also provide a way out so that you can endure it." –1 Corinthians 10:13

Through rest I'm in a better place to receive the grace of God to overcome these temptations. With enough sleep, I can more easily locate the way of escape from a sticky situation as described in 1 Corinthians 10:13.

Apart from the divine gift of downtime, I cannot fully awaken to the presence of God. Rest refreshes our physical bodies, expands our mental capacities, and increases our spiritual awareness. Below is a list of ways rest makes me more attuned to God.

As you read, place a check next to any you've noticed recently in your life.

- ☐ **I'm more likely to retain passages of Scripture I read and study.**
- ☐ **I'm more attentive to what people are really saying to me—using both verbal and nonverbal cues—to understand their deeper needs.**
- ☐ **I'm more likely to pause to consider a Christlike response to a sticky situation.**
- ☐ **I'm more ready to reorient my day to the whispers of the Holy Spirit.**

One of the most powerful ways rest awakens me to God is simply in the reminder that He is God and I am not. By taking time—even if only a portion of a day—to stop working and rest, I'm reminded that God holds all things together. Not me. Rest helps reorient my life Godward. Often when I rest, I'll awaken to a different perspective. The item or detail I thought was oh so important didn't need as much attention. But the thing I had overlooked suddenly became essential.

NOTABLE:

Rest beckons us to pull aside for a few choice moments in the middle of a hectic day to remember God's faithfulness and recognize His presence.

I find comfort in knowing that despite the countless demands on Jesus' time and the importance of His ministry, He still takes time away to rest and reconnect with God through prayer. Pulling away from the everyday demands is essential.

Why do you think Jesus chooses such a place to go to in Luke 4:42-43?

What is the result of Jesus' time in that place?

When has spending time with Jesus made you more confident in your identity or purpose?

Sometimes we can convince ourselves that unless we can get a two-week vacation or an entire weekend off we can't experience the rest, rejuvenation, and reorientation God wants to give us. But God can do amazing things with only small pockets of time.

Jesus extends the invitation to come away. In Mark 6:31, Jesus instructs His followers to "Come away by yourselves to a lonely place and rest for a while." The word *oligos* in the Greek that's translated "a while" actually means "little, small, few." I love this detail! Because it means God can do great things with only a sliver of time.

Reflecting on Mark 6:31, how is Jesus making this invitation to you right now? What's stopping you from responding?

Don't miss the invitation to come away with Christ to be renewed and restored.

CLOSING PRAYER: Spend some time asking God for opportunities to rest over the course of the upcoming week and embrace them when they arrive.

DAY THREE

THE ART OF SAYING NO

I HAVE A NIECE with the beautiful name Noellani. Her parents call her Noe for short. When she was born, I speculated what would happen when she grew older and began to speak. As expected, one of her favorite first words was, No! Like most children, she learned to say that single syllable with strength and sass. To this day, I still smile whenever she finds her voice and shouts out the word No—which is just part of her name.

Like most children, I learned the word no and used it every chance I could. But as I grew older, somewhere along the way I stopped saying no as much until it began to be a word that I didn't really want to say at all. "No" caused conflict. "No" didn't win approval. "No" became more exhausting to say than "yes" in the moment. I began responding to that little voice that said, "If you don't do this, you'll disappoint them."

On the continuum below, mark how often you say "No."

"No" is not in my vocabulary. —————————— I say "No" very often.

Circle the phrases below that best describe why you find saying "No" hard.

- **I want to be involved.**
- **I want to make a difference.**
- **I like being liked.**
- **I want to serve others.**
- **I don't want to be rude.**
- **I want to be easy to get along with.**
- **I'm afraid of conflict.**
- **I fear they won't ask again.**
- **I don't want to reject someone.**
- **I know they really need me.**

We all have that voice that tells us why we should say yes when it's not really in our best interest—or theirs either. Sometimes in saying yes to something that isn't our responsibility, we take up someone else's place and deny them the opportunity to grow, serve, and become more involved.

In not mastering the art of saying no, I ended up saying yes to countless activities and demands that weren't my responsibility. Resentment crept into my life. I began feeling used and taken advantage of. The result was burnout and exhaustion.

What kinds of situations or requests are hardest for you to say no?

Identify one thing in your life right now to which you wish you had said no. What stopped you from saying no at the time?

NOTABLE:

Luke 12:13-15 contains a hidden example of Jesus saying no to becoming a legal arbitrator. In the process, He leaves us with a rich lesson on truly living.

I know I'm not the only one who has struggled with saying no. I've noticed my friends, many of whom are time-crunched moms, offering to bake dozens of cookies they didn't have the time or energy to make, regretting and resenting their commitment. I've watched as well-meaning dads volunteered to coach their son's sports team without realizing they just sacrificed the last of their family's time to be together. I've seen some of my dearest friends, a couple in their fifties, become so overcommitted to an inspiring list of work and community development activities that they were only thinly present.

In order to change, I had to begin mastering the art of saying no. Even to this day I feel like I'm a C-student at best, but I'm still committed to growing and learning in this area (and not becoming jealous of my amazing niece who doesn't have any issues saying no).

One of the biggest lessons I've learned is that God has provided a way to prevent us from giving an automatic yes answer to whatever request comes my way—prayer.

When we take time to pray, really pray, about opportunities for involvement, and ask for wisdom concerning our time commitments, schedules, and activities, something shifts not only in our hearts but in our calendars. As we begin each day asking God to order our steps and take control of our most limited commodity—time—we find that the Holy Spirit begins leading and directing us more clearly.

NOTABLE:

John 6:26-27 is another hidden example of Jesus saying no this time to provide for the people. Jesus won't allow the people to seek what is good "bread" at the cost of what is best—"the Bread of Life."

How does David respond when given an opportunity to fight for his people in 1 Chronicles 14:8-10?

David offers a similar response in 1 Chronicles 14:11-17. How does God's response differ in verses 14-15 in comparison to verse 10?

Why is taking time to seek God's wisdom in the midst of your daily life so important?

As we pray and seek God, we will find that some of the activities and invitations we receive are ones to which we should say yes, but still others we need to respond with no. This is when we have the opportunity of mastering the art of saying no.

Here are seven principles to saying no that I've found valuable:

As you read these principles about saying no, underline (or write in the margin) some key ideas you could use to help you establish healthier boundaries.

1 **DON'T PUT OFF SAYING NO A MOMENT LONGER.** We're often tempted to avoid saying no and sense the conflict it brings. Don't wait or avoid the conversation. Though you may hope the request goes away, it rarely does.

2 **BE GRACIOUS.** Use a kind tone and gracious language in your response. Consider complimenting the person's or group's efforts by beginning with, "I really appreciate all your work and everything you're doing."

3 **WHEN YOU'RE BLINDSIDED BY A REQUEST, DON'T GIVE A KNEE-JERK REACTION.** Instead say, "Let me think about it and I'll get back to you" or explain "I'm in the middle of something, but I could connect tomorrow to hear more details." If you feel like you're being pressured on the spot, then let the person know that without time to consider the opportunity the answer is automatically no.

4 **USE DIRECT AND CLEAR LANGUAGE.** "I'm not available because of previous commitments" is a concise way to say no firmly. But if you want to be considered in the future then let them know.

5 **BE WARY OF GOING INTO ALL THE DETAILS.** Rather than offer a firm and clear no, you may be tempted to explain the extenuating circumstances that make you unavailable. Sometimes such responses begin with the innocent words, "I'd love to be a part of what you're doing but (insert series of reasons)." You do not need to give excuses for saying no.

6 **BE PREPARED TO REPEAT YOUR ANSWER.** Some people literally won't take no for an answer. When this happens, remain calm and clearly repeat your position again.

7 **REMEMBER THAT SOMETIMES THE SIMPLEST, MOST DIRECT RESPONSE IS BEST: "NO, I CAN'T."**

Now circle the one you struggle with the most to put into practice. Why do you think you struggle with it?

As we learn to master the art of saying no we have opportunity to say yes to all that God has for us. With more open spots on our calendars, we leave space for God to move, direct, and redirect us into greater service in His kingdom.

CLOSING PRAYER: Spend some time prayerfully considering what opportunity or activity in your life you need to say no to right now. Reflect on the seven principles above and courageously say no—in order to say yes to more of what God has for you.

DAY FOUR

ENGAGE IN LIFE-GIVING ACTIVITIES

FOR ME, PART OF REDISCOVERING THE WONDER of rest was realizing I had an unhealthy understanding of rest. I always thought of rest as taking a nap or getting a few extra hours of sleep. But rest isn't a purely passive activity. Rest invites us to participate in restorative activities.

Consider the following ideas regarding rest and underline any words or phrases that stand out to you:

1. **Sometimes what's most restful and restorative to you may involve activity.**
2. **Sometimes what feels like rest to you may feel like work to someone else (and vice versa).**
3. **Sometimes rest really does mean taking a nap.**
4. **Rest invites us to experience the wonder of God in new and fresh ways.**

BONUS ACTIVITY:

Pinterest is a great website for discovering fabulous creative ideas. Whether you're looking for something fresh in the kitchen or art room, you'll find a treasure trove of ideas. Join me on Pinterest at *www.pinterest.com/mafeinberg.*

Some people experience rest and rejuvenation through physical exercise, others prefer a creative outlet like painting, sculpting, or finding a project on Pinterest. Still others experience rest through spending time at the rifle range, reading an entertaining book, working on a car, enjoying a comedy, or cooking a new recipe.

When I was asked what activities made me feel the most rested and rejuvenated I responded with a blank stare. I didn't know. I worked for so long and so hard I forgot what activities brought me joy—those that made me feel most alive. I know I'm not the only who has struggled in this area.

While grabbing lunch with my dear friend Leslie, she admitted she also struggled, not only to carve out the time, but even to remember what activities rejuvenated her. With two kids, a demanding job, and an aging home that constantly needs work, she and her husband find themselves crawling in bed exhausted most nights. Yet Leslie knows that in order to give her best self to her husband, kids, and job, she needs to rediscover these things and make time for them.

We all do.

When we make time for life-giving activities, we're more sensitive to the nudges of the Holy Spirit and the grace God wants to pour in and through us.

In the space below, make a list of five activities that allow you to experience rest and rejuvenation. Then place the date of the last time you engaged in this activity.

Activity	Last Time You Engaged in This Activity
1.	
2.	
3.	
4.	
5.	

What did you discover? When I made my list, I found myself staring at the page. To be honest, I didn't have anything to write down, because, like my friend, Leslie, far too much time had passed since I'd engaged in any such activities—or at least engaged them in such a way to feel rested and rejuvenated.

But as I thought and prayed (and still continue to!) about what activities are restful and bring me joy and life, I began to compile a still-growing list.

+ BONUS ACTIVITY:

One of the ways we explored and discovered some life giving activities was by taking advantage of Groupon and Living Social coupon specials that allowed us to try new things at a discounted cost—from ziplining to securing a concealed weapons permit to taking cooking classes. Look for specials in your local paper and online to try something new. You may find yourself rejuvenated in ways you never expected!

A long walk enjoying God's creation.

Sitting at a coffee shop's patio table on a cool afternoon.

Visiting a local farmer's market.

Going to Costco with Leif.

Crawling in bed and watching an episode of one of my favorite television shows.

Curling up on the couch with a non-work related book.

Drinking iced tea on the deck with friends.

Sitting in the warm sun playing fetch with our superpup Hershey.

Walking through an art gallery or local art fair.

After identifying these life-giving activities, I needed to engage in them. But to be honest, I felt guilty. Why go to a farmer's market when I could work on the lawn or catch up on a work project or finish folding the laundry? I struggled with feeling guilty for taking care of myself.

Have you ever felt guilty for making time to care for yourself? If so, how did you respond to the sense of guilt?

What does loving your neighbor as yourself as described in Mark 12:30-31 mean for you?

Do you think you can truly love your neighbor if you don't love yourself? Explain.

Part of loving ourselves means treating ourselves with the same gentleness and kindness as we would a neighbor who has fallen ill. After all, if we don't know how to take care of ourselves, then how will we know how to care for our neighbor?

In failing to care for myself, I wasn't loving people more, but less.

When have you failed to care for yourself and found yourself caring for people less?

In embracing the fine art of rest and laughter and play, I found myself not only becoming a better neighbor but loving my neighbor more.

For too long I squeezed life-giving activities out of my schedule in the name of effectiveness, efficiency, and impact—not realizing these are the very activities that make me more effective, more efficient, and able to have a greater impact. By slowing down to embrace restful, life-giving activities, I found I was no longer operating out of exhaustion or weariness but out of life and joy.

When I carve out time to do these things, my pace slows, the fruit of the Spirit—including peace, joy, and patience—blossom in my heart. Though it seems counterintuitive, I naturally have more to give others because I'm not giving out of a sense of emptiness, but the fullness of life and the goodness of God. In this place I'm more sensitive to the Holy Spirit and more apt to discover the wonder of God in the midst of every day.

Over the course of this week, I'd like to challenge you to select one of the activities on your list that brings you rest and rejuvenation that you haven't done in a while. Make time to do the activity this week and plan to share what you experience and discover through it with the group next time you meet. And don't forget to add a few of the wonders of God you experience to your Wonderstruck Journal.

CLOSING PRAYER: Spend some time asking God to reveal other life-giving activities He has given you that help remind you who God has called and created you to be. Ask the Holy Spirit to give you the opportunities to engage in these activities—alone and with other people.

DAY FIVE

A HOLY PLACE IN SPACE AND TIME

THE SABBATH, A HOLY PLACE IN SPACE AND TIME, is a wonder-filled gift of God and one that God does not keep to Himself. In the face of relentless demands to work and produce, God stands toe-to-toe in His call to rest. God never apologizes for the Sabbath, but established the Sabbath from the beginning of time for all time. God extends His palm to all of creation and says, "Work, you can go here and no further." Without such a protest, humanity succumbs to a subtle and slippery form of slavery in which toil has no end.

Each week, God invites us to take a break for 86,400 seconds from the demands of productivity, the never-ending to-do lists, the frazzling deadlines, and simply enter His rest. The invitation is breathtaking and marvelous. And the transformation that awaits us is life changing.

+ BONUS ACTIVITY:

Check out one of my favorite books on the Sabbath, *Perspectives on the Sabbath:* 4 Views, ed. Christopher Donato, to expand your understanding of this special gift of God.

The Sabbath invites us to rest our mind, body, and souls.

The Sabbath invites us to reorder our world.

The Sabbath invites us to reorient ourselves to God.

The very first biblical reference to the Sabbath is found in Exodus. The Israelites wander through the wilderness and God sustains them with a miraculous food from heaven called *manna*, meaning "What is it?" The instructions regarding the collection of manna introduce the people to the Sabbath.

What does God's instruction regarding manna in Exodus 16:23-29 reveal about His concern for the people—beyond their physical appetites?

God gives these instructions four chapters before Moses ascends Mount Sinai. God is not only going with the people in His provision and guidance, but He is going before them.

All 10 of the commandments Moses receives atop Mount Sinai provide boundaries for God's people that empower us to live the best possible life in relation to God, each other, and all of creation. But I'd argue that there's something special about the Sabbath—not because it's the longest command, but because of its reach to so many different living things. God doesn't just command His people, but their descendants, servants, and livestock to enter His rest.

What does Exodus 20:8-11 reveal about God's concern for everything and everyone to rest?

QUOTABLE:

"Not without design does God write the music of our lives. But be it ours to learn the time and not be dismayed at the 'rests.' They are not to be slurred over, nor to be omitted, nor to destroy the melody, nor to change the keynote. If we look up, God Himself will beat time for us. With the eye on Him we shall strike the next note full and clear." -John Ruskin, artist and writer[8]

Which of those who God commands not to work listed in Exodus 20:10 surprises you the most? Why?

In the Old Testament, God didn't only create a day for the Sabbath, but an actual year. Exodus 23 describes that every seventh year the land is to lie fallow in order to allow the soil to recover.

How does Exodus 23:10-12 challenge the people to trust God more?

How does observing the Sabbath challenge you to trust God for His provision in your life?

NOTABLE:

The Sabbath isn't a rest stop along an interstate providing fuel, food, and bathroom breaks so I can drive hard the rest of the week. The Sabbath is designed to reorient all of life—including all the other 86,400 second batches during the week.

One of the great wonders of the Sabbath rest is found in how much God can do in a short amount of time. As I began creating space for rest, I began noticing areas of clutter in my life—activities and events I hadn't seen before that needed to be cut. I also found that many of the big concerns I carried into a day of rest became right-sized. And in rest, I could no longer measure my worth or value by productivity. I once again had to turn to God.

Setting apart time to enter into rest, I became more attuned to God's presence and voice.

Though Scripture reading has always been an important spiritual discipline in my life, for months the practice felt all discipline, void of anything spiritual. I felt as though I were reading an instruction manual backwards—nothing connected or made any sense. Then one morning, sitting on the couch with coffee in hand, I flipped open the pages of my well-worn Bible and stumbled on the words of Paul, "I can do all things through Christ who strengthens me" (Philippians 4:13, NKJV).

I'd read the passage countless times before, but this time the words reverberated in my soul—no longer Paul's expression but my own. Ruminating on this passage, I sensed God reminding me that His supernatural strength and power are available upon request. Energy surged through my veins as I prayed, infusing my spirit. I felt spiritually awake and alert for the first time in as long as I could remember.

Over the following weeks, the Bible came alive each day like a pop-up book, and I became more sensitive to the sacred echoes all around me. The wonder of Sabbath was alive in me.

Reflecting on Hebrews 4:9-11, how can you be more intentional about entering the rest God wants to give you?

NOTABLE:

The Sabbath was not created as a day filled with stifling rules and guidelines, but as a gift from God to His beloved people. The Sabbath was not designed as something to be dreaded, but as a time to eagerly anticipate.

One of the wonders of Sabbath is that the holy place in time and space is always unfolding before us—beckoning us to come away from the busyness of life to simply be with Christ. In this place, we find ourselves renewed, rejuvenated, and more full of God and the life He's designed for us. So don't wait—enter the Sabbath, celebrate the Sabbath, and savor the Sabbath every chance you receive.

I pray that God is filling you with well-needed rest and rejuvenation as you continue to be wonderstruck by the Creator. My hope is that beginning now, you set a new pattern of celebrating rest in your life—thanking God for the gift each day. May the Lord fill you with His presence, encourage you with His hope, and guide you with His love.

You won't want to miss next week as we dive into the wonder of prayer. We're going to explore the prayers of Jesus, wrestle with God's silence, and look at some of the challenges of developing and maintaining a vibrant prayer life as well as some practical ideas to help you grow in your communication with God.

CLOSING PRAYER: Spend some time asking God how you can set aside a day or two half days or weave together several partial days off to develop a rhythm of rest in your life.

THE WONDER OF PRAYER

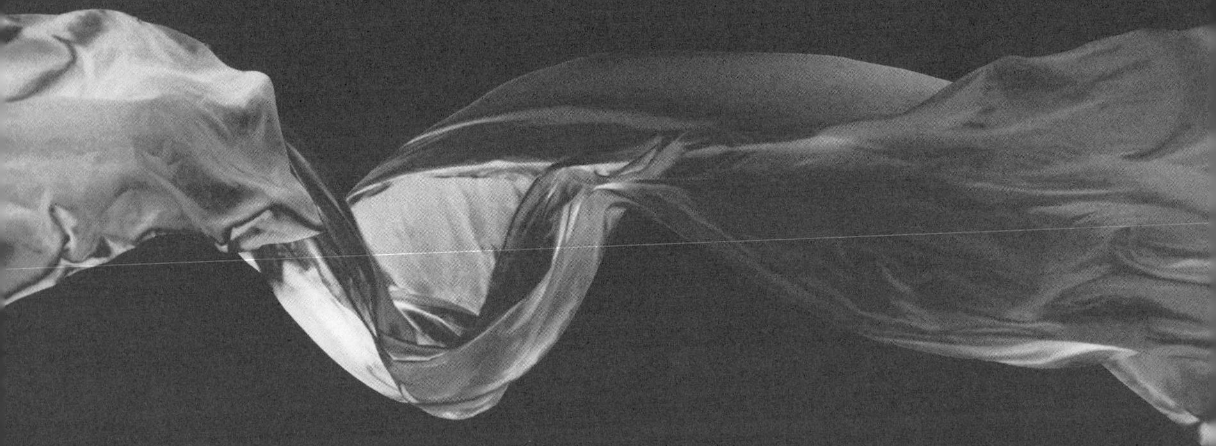

SESSION FOUR

GROUP GETTING STARTED: (10-15 minutes)

SESSION FOUR: THE WONDER OF PRAYER

HOMEWORK GROUP DISCUSSION

1 Ask participants to share three moments they recorded in the Wonderstruck Journal on page 163 in which they encountered the wonder of God and His handiwork this week.

2 In Day One's homework, you were asked to prayerfully examine your own calendar. Describe any changes you resolved to make regarding bedtimes, wake times, downtimes, exercise or otherwise. How are you experiencing the wonder of rest in your life since you began making those changes?

3 On page 68 in Day Three's homework, you were asked to circle phrases that best described why saying no is difficult for you. Which phrases did you circle? Through the lesson, what activities did you recognize you need to withdraw from or say no to in order to say yes to more of the wonders God has for you?

4 During the homework for Day Four, you were challenged to select one of the activities on your list that brings you rest and rejuvenation that you haven't done in a while and make time for it. What activity did you choose? How did the activity remind you of who and Whose you are?

5 Reflecting on the final day's homework, what are you doing in your life to enter the holy place in space and time?

EXPERIENTIAL ACTIVITY: SAVORING PRAYER

WHAT YOU'LL NEED:

- A variety of 3-5 fresh fruits and/or sweet and salty snacks
- Small plates, napkins, forks

1 Invite each participant to take at least one of each item, recognizing that some people won't be able to select items because of food allergies.

2 Then invite the participants to take time to thank God for every person involved in making each item on the plate—including the plate. This may include the person who prepared the soil for growing the strawberry, the person who watered the seed, the person who fought off pests so the strawberry could grow, as well as those who picked, prepared, packaged, transported, stocked, sold, and made the strawberry available to eat today. These prayers of thanksgiving can continue for every person involved with each item. This prayer time will take several minutes.

3 Then invite participants to slowly eat the same item at the same time and comment on the particulars about the food—texture, flavor, saltiness, sweetness, bitterness, and so forth—that they haven't noticed in a while and offer their appreciation. For example, "thank You, God, for making strawberries so sweet."

4 Discuss the following questions:

How fast do you normally pray over a meal: Speedily, steadily, or slowly?

What did you learn or discover as you slowed down and prayed for all the people involved in making the food available for you?

How does slowing the rate of prayer affect how you pray? what you pray for? your attitude toward God?

PLAY THE SESSION FOUR VIDEO: [18:30]

NOTES

VIDEO DISCUSSION

1 What are the top three things that prevent you from praying more?

2 How have you been praying it safe in your prayer life?

3 How much are you really saying to God when you pray?

4 After watching the video and reading Matthew 6:9-13, what stands out to you most from The Lord's Prayer?

5 Read Matthew 6:7. Where have "nonversations" replaced conversation in your prayers?

6 What slight shifts in your prayer life could reignite your relationship with God?

CLOSING PRAYER

- As you close in prayer ask:
- that each person's heart, mind, and life awaken to a greater sense of God's wonder
- God to give each participant a renewed desire to go deeper and further in prayer
- the Holy Spirit to illuminate any areas where participants have been holding back in their prayer lives.

DAY ONE

THE MYSTERY OF PRAYER

THIS WEEK:

If you are following along in the trade book, read chapter, ".005: Forgotten Longings" and ".006: Treasure Hunting in Africa," and tackle the five days of homework to prepare for the next gathering.

BONUS ACTIVITY:

Spend time committing Romans 12:12 to memory this week. You'll find a flash card on page 177.

WE ALL NEED TO become more intentional about prayer, selective about our words, ready to meet our Abba Father in the syllables and the silence that emerge. The wonder of prayer is rediscovered in Who we're speaking to. Prayer is a mystical event by which we get to talk to the Creator of all—the One who fashioned our world with a few words—knowing that God not only listens but answers.

Sometime ago someone asked me why I tackled the topic of prayer in so much of my writing.

"Do I?" I responded.

In whatever I write, I'm passionate about introducing people to the wonder of God and the Scripture. That's the heartbeat behind everything I do. But as I thought back, I realized prayer often emerged as a theme. The very first book I wrote, *God Whispers: Learning to Hear His Voice* and later *The Sacred Echo: Hearing God's Voice in Every Area of Your Life*, tackled the theme of prayer head-on. I mentally thumbed through other books and Bible studies I've developed. Each one had a reference, a chapter, a story that examined a different facet of prayer.

"I think I keep coming back to prayer simply because it's my lifeline to God," I answered.

Yet despite the importance of prayer in my life, I admit on many days I find myself more frustrated than fulfilled. Sometimes I struggle for words to express what I'm thinking or feeling. Sometimes the words seem rote and tired. Sometimes I say, Amen, and quietly wonder, *Did God hear anything I said?*

I need to be reawakened to the wonder of prayer.

Through prayer we are given access to approach the One who created all things and holds all things together—a breathtaking invitation, indeed. Not only does God give us a voice, but He invites us to use that voice with Him anytime, anywhere. God eagerly awaits every request, heart cry, desire, and expression of gratitude. No syllable, consonant, or vowel offered up in prayer escapes God's notice. Yet despite the opportunity to bend the ear of God, many of us struggle with how we should pray, what we should say, and what a vibrant prayer life really looks and feels like.

I recently asked my friends on Facebook to honestly share what the toughest part of prayer is for them. As you read these statements about prayer, mark any you also struggle with.

- ☐ "Finding a place to pray with no distractions." –Kelly
- ☐ "Praying selflessly." –Paul
- ☐ "The hardest is praying when I'm mad or upset." –Melissa
- ☐ "Not seeing the answer in the way I want or in my time." –Goldie
- ☐ "Believing I'm worthy of a response." –Jamie
- ☐ "Staying focused." –Tammy
- ☐ "Praying with others or aloud." –Bill
- ☐ "When I find a quiet place, I find my head nodding in sleep." –Sandy
- ☐ "Keeping the momentum to pray everyday." –Sheryl
- ☐ "Confessing and accepting forgiveness. I know God knows, but offering it up makes it more real and awful." –Rachel
- ☐ "Allowing it to be sincere, not something I'm trying to cross off my to-do list." –Carly
- ☐ "Unanswered prayers become hurtful." –Carole

BONUS ACTIVITY:

You can connect with Margaret on Facebook at *www.facebook.com/margaretfeinberg*. Drop her a note and make her day!

Circle the one you struggle with the most in your prayer life right now. Why do you think you struggle with it?

To be honest, I've struggled with all of these.

Prayer is simply communicating with God. Through prayer, we both listen and talk to God. Despite the simplicity of prayer, I've spent many years struggling to develop a rhythm of prayer in my life.

I created a prayer journal—which I lost. I started a scrapbook prayer book—which I never finished. My efforts at creating prayer lists soon disappeared—along with the paper they were written on. As much as I wanted to develop a vibrant prayer life, I struggled to find a method that helped anchor me to some form of consistency.

QUOTABLE:

"You will seek me and find me when you seek me with all your heart." –Jeremiah 29:13

Have you struggled to develop a consistent rhythm of prayer in your life?

If so, how specifically have you struggled?

My Facebook friends gave some really helpful responses when I asked what they've done to help develop a more consistent rhythm of prayer. Highlight any ideas that might be helpful in your prayer life.

- ☐ "I try to never get out of bed without talking to God. It's become a habit and now usually happens before I even open my eyes." –Leah

- ☐ "I keep a journal that records requests, when I begin praying, and when they are answered. In those discouraging times, I can look back and see where God has answered." –Julie

- ☐ "Every time I look at the clock and see 1:11 or 2:22 or anytime like that. I could be home, in a car, at the office, and it's a good reminder (to pray)." –Misty

- ☐ **"(I) form habits with my kids. They unknowingly hold me accountable with bedtime prayers and meal prayers. My eldest and I just started keeping a journal together. We pray after we both make entries." –Alexandra**

- ☐ **"I adopted a snooze prayer method this year. I set my alarm 10 minutes or so before I have to get up. When the alarm goes off, I hit snooze and instead of rolling over and going back to sleep, I roll over and begin praying. A pretty wondrous way to start the day." –Ann**

- ☐ **"Teenage children with drivers' licenses keep me praying." –Del**

- ☐ **"As I read Scripture, I ask God where He is working, and how I can join Him there. Praying the Scripture works for me." –Robin**

- ☐ **"Journaling helps me stay focused, gives my hands something to do, and reveals things to me I didn't even realize!" –Valorie**

NOTABLE:

Prayer comes in many forms including petition, confession, adoration, love, intercessions, praise, meditation, and thanksgiving.

Frustrated by my lack of consistency, I decided to create a prayer list on some of the blank sheets in the back of my Bible. Something about those pages made the list feel more permanent and didn't require an extra book or journal to carry around.

I began by creating a rough draft on a blank sheet of paper and prayerfully considered each entry for a few days. Then I carefully transferred many of the names and requests to the back of my Bible. When I finished reading the Scriptures each day I could easily flip to the back of my Bible.

What have you found to be helpful in developing a steady rhythm in your prayer life?

I made that list more than 10 years ago and I've continued praying for each of those people, offering up various petitions. The list includes family members, friends, neighbors, acquaintances, political leaders, as well as personal petitions for areas I want to grow more fully in God. My guess is that there are people on this list who would be surprised to know I've been praying for them regularly for so many years.

Who do you pray for regularly that would be surprised to know you pray for them?

QUOTABLE:

"We learn to praise God not by paying compliments but by paying attention. Watch how the trees exult when the wind is in them. Mark the utter stillness of the great blue heron in the swamp. Listen to the sound of the rain. Learn how to say Hallelujah from the ones who say it." –Frederick Buechner, biblical scholar[9]

At the top of my prayer list are the words "adoration" and "praise," because I like to begin each prayer time by expressing affection and gratitude to God simply for who He is—apart from anything He's done. Then I begin moving through the list. Sometimes slowly. Sometimes fast. Some days I pray for only those listed and conclude with "Amen." But other days the list serves as a launching pad for praying for many other people and situations.

If I'm honest, some days the prayer list feels like a list. I bulldoze through and feel nothing at all. Other days I look at the same list and each name is vibrant, alive as the syllables ascend from my lips. I still don't know what makes the difference, and I think that's part of the mystery of prayer. But what I do know is that having this list anchors me in my prayer life.

When I don't know what to say or don't feel like praying, I come back to this list. Years have passed. Though I still see people's names who have yet to know Christ and prayers that haven't been answered in the ways I hope or long for, I see other names and requests God has answered in profound ways. One such example is the listed husband of a friend who wanted nothing to do with Jesus a few years ago. Now he's passionate about his faith and making sure all of his friends hear the incredible news of what God is doing in his life. Such remembrances encourage me to pray and keep praying.

What prayers have you seen answered in the last five years that encourage you to pray and keep praying?

BONUS ACTIVITY:

Don't forget to continue adding moments where you've been wonderstruck by God in your Wonderstruck Journal on page 162.

What encouragement does 1 John 5:14 provide you in your prayer life right now?

I'm still in the beginning stages of understanding prayer, plying its depths, and laying hold of God. In the next few days of homework, we're going to dive into nine prayers Jesus prayed in the Gospels. I continue the journey with great expectation and hope you'll continue to make the journey, too.

CLOSING PRAYER: Spend some time reflecting on your current rhythm of prayer. Prayerfully consider what changes you could make—in your schedule, your approach, your attitude—that would nurture your desire and ability to call out to God more frequently.

DAY TWO

THE PRAYER OF JESUS

IN A NEIGHBORHOOD KNOWN as the Highlands on the outskirts of Denver is a red brick restaurant known as Spuntino's, which means "little snack" in Italian. While they're renowned for paninis and pastas, Leif and I have become avid fans of their Popsicles. Made in-house from an unusual blend of natural juices, fruits, and spices, the nontraditional flavors include roasted red pepper, basil, and balsamic as well as the jaw-dropping delicious French toast. I'm a fan of their celery and lime as well as their black pepper melon.

BONUS ACTIVITY:

Taking a trip to Denver soon? Stop by Spuntino's and see for yourself. *www.spuntinodenver.com*

On our first visit, one of the co-owners showed us the magical machine that spits out these delightful treats, a specialty Popsicle freezer imported from Brazil. The secret: The contraption freezes Popsicles in 18 minutes so ice crystals don't have time to form. The result is a creamy, dreamy delight that keeps us coming back on sizzling summer days. The selection changes steadily as new combinations are conceived and created. Only a chef with an artisan's heart could make something as mundane as a Popsicle extraordinary.

One of the most surprising aspects of these scrumptious Popsicles is the simplicity of the ingredients. Just a few items are needed—puréed fruit or vegetables, an unexpected spice, and a dollop of sugar to create something unforgettable.

My hunch is that the disciples are surprised by the simplicity of ingredients, or at least the few words Jesus uses when He instructs them on prayer. In Luke 11, one of the disciples asks Jesus how to pray. He answers with a prayer marked by simplicity, brevity, and profundity. A slightly longer form of the prayer is recorded in Matthew 6.

Eugene Peterson offers a fresh reading of this familiar prayer, which is often called The Lord's Prayer. Underline anything that stands out to you as you read this modern portrayal of The Lord's Prayer. Which word or ideas are most meaningful in your life right now? Why?

"Our Father in heaven, Reveal who you are. Set the world right; Do what's best—as above, so below. Keep us alive with three square meals. Keep us forgiven with you and forgiving others. Keep us safe from ourselves and the Devil. You're in charge! You can do anything you want! You're ablaze in beauty! Yes. Yes. Yes." –Matthew 6:9-13, MSG

When asked how to pray, Jesus provides a specific prayer as a model. This was common in the time period. Rabbis of the day customarily gave their disciples prayers they could use habitually. The early church offered this prayer three times a day following the ancient Jewish rhythm of prayer: morning, afternoon, and evening.

Here is the same prayer in more familiar language.

"Our ______ Father who is in heaven, Hallowed be Your name. Your kingdom come. Your will be done, On earth as it is in heaven. Give us this day our daily bread. And forgive us our debts, as we also have forgiven our debtors. And do not lead us into temptation, but deliver us from evil." –Matthew 6:9-13 NASB

The prayer begins with the word "Our"—a powerful reminder that as we approach God it's not just about us. We're part of a larger community of God's children.

When you approach God in prayer, do you tend to think in terms of "my" or "our"?

How does your approach affect the way you interact with God and others?

NOTABLE:

Matthew continually emphasizes the importance of the kingdom of God throughout his Gospel. This prayer not only describes the kingdom on earth ushered in by Jesus, but also the final kingdom—free from sin and death.

BONUS ACTIVITY:

Please personalize the prayers this week by writing *abba* in the blanks beside each occurrence of the word *Father.*

NOTABLE:

Jesus lived in a culture of multiple languages. The people He grew up with spoke Aramaic, but written documents were primarily in Greek. The Greek word for *father* in the New Testament is *pater*, but Jesus would have spoken the Aramaic word *abba*.

NOTABLE:

God can be described as both immanent and transcendent: immanent which identifies God's nearness and transcendent which identifies God's complete sovereignty over creation.

The prayer continues with the word Father. When Jesus chooses to address God in this way, He issues an invitation that we, too, can approach God as our Heavenly Dad in a relationship marked by intimacy and affection. Jesus acknowledges our *Abba* is in heaven. This doesn't mean God is far off, withdrawn, or remote, but that the divine otherness of God is preserved. In other words, God is both intimately involved and yet above and beyond everything we can wrap our minds around.

Do you tend to approach God in prayer as your Dad? Why or why not?

How does your understanding of God in this way affect the way you pray?

QUOTABLE:

"To hallow God's name is to set it apart in our hearts and in our minds and on our lips, to set it apart and make it holy. It is to regard the name of God as the truest and dearest, highest and holiest of all names." –Stephen Shoemaker, author and pastor[10]

The Lord's Prayer can be divided into two sets of three petitions. The first set of petitions is concerned with God:

Hallowed be Your name.

Your kingdom come.

Your will be done on earth as it is in heaven.

These short statements acknowledge that beyond the borders of our wildest imaginations, God resides in splendor unspeakable. Though our physical eyes can't perceive this heavenly kingdom, God, in His brilliance, is above our comprehension.

In asking for God's will to be unleashed, we're asking God to release His glory, to reign into every cranny of creation—including us. Making the plea requires us to trust in greater measure the goodness and lovingkindness of God as we conform our longings to God's desires. We cannot pray these words without trusting the holy, loving nature of God. But when we're audacious enough to lift these three petitions to God—calling for His holiness, kingdom, and will—we're asking God to fulfill His desire for all creation today and forever.

In what areas of your life do you need to experience more of God's holiness, kingdom, and will?

NOTABLE:

Jesus reminds us to trust God with our every need in Matthew 6:25-28.

The Lord's Prayer consists of a second set of three petitions that concern us. These include:

Give us today our daily bread.

Forgive us our sins as we forgive those who sin against us.

Save us in the time of temptation and deliver us from evil.

The Lord's Prayer begins with a focus on God before moving to our own needs and concerns.

When you pray, do you tend to begin with your focus on God or yourself?

How does beginning with a focus on God change your perspective and attitude in prayer?

These three petitions invite us to bring our most basic needs to God. The request for bread reminds of our need for God to provide all things—even food. We do not have to live in a grasping way, but we can come to God openhanded to receive from Him as our loving *Abba*.

Scholars note a peculiarity in the text translated, "Give us this day our daily bread." While clear that "this day" means we are asking for today's provision and not a retirement plan, the problem emerges with the word translated as "daily." In the Greek, the word is *epiousous*, but the word is rarely used.

QUOTABLE:

"Last week, while at prayer, I suddenly discovered—or felt as if I did—that I had really forgiven someone I have been trying to forgive for over thirty years. Trying, and praying that I might." –C.S. Lewis, author and theologian[12]

A famous church father named Origen, popular during the third century, noted that he couldn't find the word used among the Greeks and suggested Jesus created the word. Whatever the reasoning, the word remains a mysterious curiosity. One of my favorite solutions comes from a second-century translation that means, "Give us today the bread that doesn't run out." In many ways this expresses the heartbeat of the petition that indicates both a daily dependence on God and the call to faith for God to provide. Thus the prayer is an invitation to live continually dependent on God.[11]

The prayer reminds us of our desperate need for forgiveness. Just as we can die from lack of bread, we can also die from lack of forgiveness. Apart from forgiveness, we will starve relationally and spiritually. Yet laying hold of the fullness of God's forgiveness requires us to forgive others. The third petition suggests that no one is immune from temptation. The devil is an equal opportunity tempter. Yet through the power of God no temptation exists that we can't overcome.

NOTABLE:

The Greek word *peirasmos* meaning "temptation" can also be translated as "test" or "trial."

In what areas of your life do you need to ask God for the strength to overcome temptation?

If the first set of petitions focuses on the goodness and grandness of God, this second set of petitions highlights our dependence and need for God. The prayer encompasses both the transcendence (greatness) and immanence (nearness) of God and serves a powerful reminder that we are not the hub but merely a spoke. Everything revolves around God and we must seek Him as center of our lives.

On the continuum below, mark what you tend to focus on most when praying:

I focus on the transcendence of God (greatness).	I focus on the immanence of God (nearness).

Why is having a healthy appreciation for both important as you approach God in prayer?

NOTABLE:
Don't miss Session Six when we'll dive deeper into the transforming power of forgiveness.

The Lord's Prayer invites us to call on God in all His splendor and glory—to unleash Himself in our world. The prayer invites us to re-center our lives on the foundational truth that God is Lord of all. He is the source of provision, protection, and forgiveness. We do not have to grasp; God holds everything together.

CLOSING PRAYER: Spend some time reflecting on the words of The Lord's Prayer. Then pray each word of the prayer. Slowly. Deliberately. Out loud.

DAY THREE

THE PRAYER LIFE OF CHRIST

ONE OF THE THINGS THAT STRIKES ME about Jesus is, despite His passion in leaving to pray, the vast majority of His prayers recorded in Scripture—including the Lord's Prayer—are brief. During today's homework, I want to look at four specific prayers from Jesus' life and ministry. The first is found in the Gospel of Matthew, and the rest are found in the Gospel of John.

The first prayer is found in Matthew 11 and records Jesus offering praise to *Abba*. Jesus speaks to the Father after condemning the Galilean cities for their unbelief. He thanks and praises God for revealing the truth to His followers and keeping it from the prideful:

BONUS ACTIVITY:

Please personalize the prayers this week by writing *Abba* in the blanks beside each occurrence of the word *Father*.

> "I praise you, ______ Father, Lord of heaven and earth, because you have hidden these things from the wise and learned, and revealed them to little children. Yes, ______ Father, for this is what you were pleased to do."
> –Matthew 11:25-26

Why do you think Jesus took such pleasure in the reversal of expectations?

What does Jesus' prayer reveal about His heart for humanity?

What hope does Jesus' prayer give you right now?

The Greek word for infant, *nepiois*, (pronounced NAY-pee-ois) refers to "little ones." This includes the poor, the weak, the simple, the uneducated, and those in need. Jesus offers praise because He knows God is using unexpected, unknown people to bring forth His will.

Who are the *nepiois* God used in your life to strengthen your walk with Christ?

How is God using you as *nepiois* to reveal His love and presence to others?

The second prayer from Jesus' life and ministry I wanted to highlight comes from John 11. Jesus learns His close friend Lazarus is dead. Both Martha and Mary are devastated and disappointed that Jesus didn't come sooner. Jesus approaches the tomb and asks that the stone be removed. Martha protests. The stench will prove overwhelming. Jesus insists that if only they believe, God's glory will be revealed. Then Jesus raises His eyes. Notice He doesn't close His eyes or bow His head. Looking up to the heavens, He prays loudly so everyone can hear:

> "______ Father, I thank you that you have heard me. I knew that you always hear me, but I said this for the benefit of the people standing here, that they may believe that you sent me." –John 11:41-42

NOTABLE:

The posture Jesus takes looking open-eyed toward the heavens was common during the first century.

Again, Jesus calls out to *Abba*, His Dad. Jesus offers a prayer of thanksgiving. The words reveal the deep intimacy Jesus feels with God as well as the confidence with which He approaches God. This prayer reminds us that God's ear is tilted toward us.

On the continuum below, mark how much confidence you feel as you approach God.

I'm hesitant to approach God. — I can confidently approach God.

On the continuum below, mark how much confidence you have that God hears you as you pray.

I wonder if God really hears me. — I know God hears me and will answer.

What does John 11:41-42 reveal about the amount of confidence God wants you to experience in knowing He's with and hears you?

After Jesus prays in John 11, Lazarus waddles out from the grave. Some witnesses can't believe their eyes and put their trust in Jesus. Others plot Jesus' death. Jesus' prayer was heard.

In the third prayer I want to highlight, Jesus appears in John 12 as He enters Jerusalem shortly before His death. The petition runs parallel to the one Jesus makes in Mark 14:35-36 when He is in Gethsemane before the crucifixion. After being anointed for burial in Bethany, Jesus wrestles with God in prayer and receives an audible response from Him:

> "Now my soul is troubled, and what shall I say,' ______ Father, save me from this hour'? No, it was for this very reason I came to this hour. ______ Father, glorify your name!" –John 12:27-28

NOTABLE:

John 12 marks a transitional period in the Gospel of John. The first 12 chapters describe the signs of Jesus as the Messiah, but the last half records the ultimate glory of Jesus. Bible scholars call chapters 1-12 the Book of Signs and 13-21 the Book of Glory.

What parallels do you see between this prayer and The Lord's Prayer found in Matthew 6:9-13?

What are some areas you're struggling in to choose God's will over your will? What role is prayer playing in helping you make the best choice?

NOTABLE:

Throughout John's Gospel, we're reminded that Jesus' time has not yet come (2:4; 7:30; 8:20), but in His prayer in John 12, Jesus welcomes the coming hour. The hour being referred to is the "hour of glorification." Jesus' ministry is finished, and now He must endure the cross.

The final prayer in today's homework is known as the High Priestly Prayer. This is Jesus' longest recorded prayer. He offers the prayer in front of the disciples in the upper room as part of His Farewell Discourse. This passage is considered the beloved chapter because of the intimate look at the heart behind Jesus' life and ministry. Again, Jesus lifts His eyes to heaven and calls on *Abba*.

What does Jesus seem most concerned with when praying on the night of His arrest in John 17?

The central focus in this passage is captured in a single verse whereby, again, Jesus calls out to Abba:

> "Holy ______ Father, protect them by the power of your name, the name you gave me, so that they may be one as we are one."
> –John 17:11

Jesus' prayer is reminiscent of a petition from The Lord's Prayer; "Hallowed be Your name." But the prayer's focus is on unity. Just as no division or separation is between the Son and the Father, Jesus asks that the same supernatural ability to act with one mind, will, and purpose be given to His followers.

NOTABLE:

The Farewell Discourse recorded in John 14-17 reminds many scholars of Moses' farewell in Deuteronomy 32–33.

In what areas of your life are you experiencing the gift of unity?

In what areas of your life are you experiencing disunity, separation, or estrangement?

In the space below, write a prayer asking God to bring unity in these areas of your life.

Reflecting on the four prayers mentioned in today's homework, note each prayer contains some of the same words, "Abba" and variations of the petitions found in The Lord's Prayer. Jesus didn't only give the disciples The Lord's Prayer, He demonstrated the prayer through His life and the way He spoke to the Father.

CLOSING PRAYER: Spend time paraphrasing The Lord's Prayer in your own words. Offer up the prayer for the specific needs and issues you're currently facing in your life.

DAY FOUR

FINAL WORDS FROM THE CROSS

I RECENTLY SAT IN A CHAPEL GAZING at an image of Jesus hanging from the cross. I reflected on the suffering and pain He endured, and found myself awestruck by how exposed Jesus was in those final moments. Stripped of His clothing, Jesus' body wasn't the only thing on display. Everything about Christ—His willingness to become a sacrifice, His title as God's Son, His love for the world—was revealed for the whole world to see.

I can't quite explain why, but when I read the prayers Jesus says with His arms stretched wide on the cross, I can't help but lean in a little closer. In these final moments, what does Jesus say to the Father?

The first prayer is shocking at first glance, and yet wildly consistent with Jesus' identity and mission. His words call us back, again, to a petition found in The Lord's Prayer:

> "______ Father, forgive them, for they do not know what they are doing." –Luke 23:34

What does this prayer reveal about Jesus' capacity for forgiveness?

How does this prayer challenge you to expand your capacity for forgiveness?

The second prayer is shrouded in mystery:

> "Eli, Eli, lema sabachthani?" (which means "My God, my God, why have you forsaken me?") –Matthew 27: 46

Martin Luther was said to have sat down to prepare a sermon on this text. After spending hours examining the passage, Luther threw his hands up and exclaimed, "God forsaken by God—who can understand it?" The passage left the brilliant theologian speechless.

Indeed, the statement is hard to wrap our heads and hearts around.

Jesus begins by crying out, not with the intimate term "Father," but cries out to God twice, doubling the profound sense of alienation. The words wail and groan in their expression. For a brief moment, Jesus is no longer the Son in whom God is pleased (Matthew 3:17), but One carrying the stockpile of sin for all humanity.

When have you felt abandoned by God? How did you respond?

What comfort do you find in knowing that Jesus understands what abandonment by God feels like?

What elements of this prayer are consistent with the prophesy found in Isaiah 53:3-5?

NOTABLE:

Acts 7:59-60 records two of the prayers Stephen offered before his martyrdom, which echo the prayers of Jesus from the cross.

The prayer Jesus offers from the cross is His final prayer. Even in Jesus' final moment, Jesus reveals His heart by speaking audibly:

"______ Father, into your hands I commit my spirit." –Luke 23:46

The prayer is intensely personal and marked by full submission to God. Jesus endured the physical, emotional, and spiritual pain of the cross willingly. To the very end, Jesus voluntarily gave up His life (John 10:17-18).

> "The reason my Father loves me is that I lay down my life—only to take it up again. No one takes it from me, but I lay it down of my own accord. I have authority to lay it down and authority to take it up again. This command I received from my Father."
> –John 10:17-18

What is one obstacle in your life that you need to commit into God's hands?

BONUS ACTIVITY:

To better set the context for Jesus' prayers on the cross, rent or borrow a copy of *The Passion of the Christ*.

What does surrendering or relinquishing all you are and all you love to God each day look like for you?

Aramaic was the commonly spoken language of Jesus' day. Mark 14:36 shows us that Jesus addressed God as His *Abba* Father. This experience of knowing God as *Abba*, a name of both intimacy and respect, didn't only shape the prayers, but the life and ministry of Christ.

How much more should it shape ours?

BONUS ACTIVITY:

Use *www.biblegateway.com* or a concordance to look up the word "forsaken" in the Scripture. Note how many times the word appears and the deepness of the cry of those who feel forsaken.

CLOSING PRAYER: Spend some time asking God to reveal Himself as your Abba Father and to infuse you with His love. As you pray throughout today, consider addressing God as Abba Father and live awake to the way God may want to reveal His presence to you.

DAY FIVE

PERSISTENCE WITH GOD

AS THE DISCIPLES WATCH JESUS walk in the power and presence of God, they become more than intrigued by Jesus' prayer life. They want to pray like Jesus. In His love, Jesus gives them a backstage pass to see how and when He prays. At times, He even prays aloud so the disciples can hear His requests. I imagine the disciples hang on every word and live wide-eyed to how Jesus lives out a life of prayer.

In the chart below, match the passage with what the disciples witness in Jesus' prayer life. Place a star by the passage about Jesus' prayer life that's most meaningful to you right now.

Jesus prays for others	**Matthew 26:36-44**
Jesus prays with others	**Matthew 14:23**
Jesus prays alone	**Luke 6:12**
Jesus prays outside	**Luke 9:28**
Jesus prays regularly	**Matthew 19:13**
Jesus knows not all of His prayers will be answered as desired	**Luke 5:16**

NOTABLE:

The apostle Paul often exhorts believers to persist in prayer in passages such as Romans 12:12, Ephesians 6:18, and Colossians 4:2.

For me, I placed a star by the idea that Jesus knows that not all of His prayers will be answered as desired. Jesus asks that the cup of suffering be removed from Him, but doesn't receive what He desires. Instead, He willingly submits to God's desire above His own. This moment in Jesus' prayer life reminds me of all the times I've prayed and not received the answer I wanted. Yet despite this, Jesus repeatedly encourages us to persist in prayer.

NOTABLE:
In ancient Jewish culture, hospitality was held in high regard, as almost a duty. A dilemma arises when a host has no food for his guest, and he approaches a neighbor for help.

Jesus provides the disciples with a model for prayer in The Lord's Prayer. Whereas Matthew's Gospel describes a sermon-like setting when introducing The Lord's Prayer, Luke's Gospel introduces it amidst a series of teachings about relating to God. Then Jesus goes on to teach a parable on the importance of being audacious in our requests to God.

What is the most important thing Jesus is trying to communicate about prayer following The Lord's Prayer in Luke 11:5-13?

What are three reasons you're tempted to give up praying?

-
-
-

When has persevering in prayer as a follower of Jesus been hardest for you?

Persistence in prayer isn't only about making the same request to God repeatedly, but about continuing to grow in our prayer lives—even when God doesn't answer in the way we expect. As we pray, we can walk in the confidence that God will give us the mercy, grace, and strength we need to endure whatever we must face.

NOTABLE:

Jesus' parable says the judge feared the woman wearing him out. The Greek expression for being "worn out" by someone is the same phrase used to describe giving a black eye.[13]

I find comfort that Jesus knew we'd sometimes be tempted to give up on praying. He knew we'd look at our world and the countless injustices, the overwhelming brokenness, the hardness of human hearts, and consider throwing up our hands and walking away. Yet Jesus challenges us to pray and keep on praying. Prayer isn't merely an expression of faith, but through prayer, faith expands in our hearts and lives.

Just like the persistent neighbor in Luke 11, another woman's persistence and boldness is used to describe our attitude in prayer. Luke 18 describes two identifiable characters: a helpless widow and a proud, independent judge. Widows were considered helpless to an ancient Jewish society. With no one left to provide for them, they were left to fend for themselves. Jesus' parable begs the question: If a coldhearted judge will answer the cries of someone in need, how much more would a loving God offer?

How is God different from the cold judge found in Luke 18:1-8?

Why is an understanding of God as a loving Abba Father so important to a healthy prayer life?

What's one area of your life or person that you've given up praying for?

How does Luke 18:1-8 challenge you to persevere in prayer?

QUOTABLE:

"The Lord watches over the foreigner and sustains the fatherless and the widow, but he frustrates the ways of the wicked." –Psalm 146:9

The persistence Jesus calls us to isn't only about asking, seeking, and knocking to receive a particular result. The persistence goes deeper as we continue to seek God in how to ask, how to seek, and how to knock. In other words, we need to persevere not just in the consistency of our petitions, but in learning to become people whose prayers are marked by increasing faith, humility, harmony with the will of God, and thanksgiving.

As we continue to pray, we may find our requests aren't answered in the way we initially thought. An illness may not be healed. People may not recognize Jesus as their Savior. Fears may not be fully stilled. Financial challenges may still loom. But through persistent prayer, we notice a change in our hearts. Through our communication with God, He draws our hearts nearer to His. We are no longer praying for our will to be done, but for God's will to be done.

Prayer is still a mystery to me. I may never understand why God decides to say yes to some of my requests, and no to others, but I sit in awe of what God does when people pray. Through prayer, my petitions, pleas, and praises are heard and my heart becomes more sensitive to the things of God.

My dear friend, you aren't going to want to miss the next session. If you're like me, if there's one thing I can't live without (besides a sugar free vanilla latte and a good steak and potato every so often), it's friendships. Whether you struggle holding onto friendships or you're someone who makes friends at every turn, you won't want to miss the next session when we'll dive into the wonders of friendship.

CLOSING PRAYER: Spend time reflecting on prayers that you used to pray. Ask God to reveal any He wants you to begin praying again. Ask for the grace and strength to persevere in prayer where you haven't received the answer you desired.

THE WONDER OF FRIENDSHIP

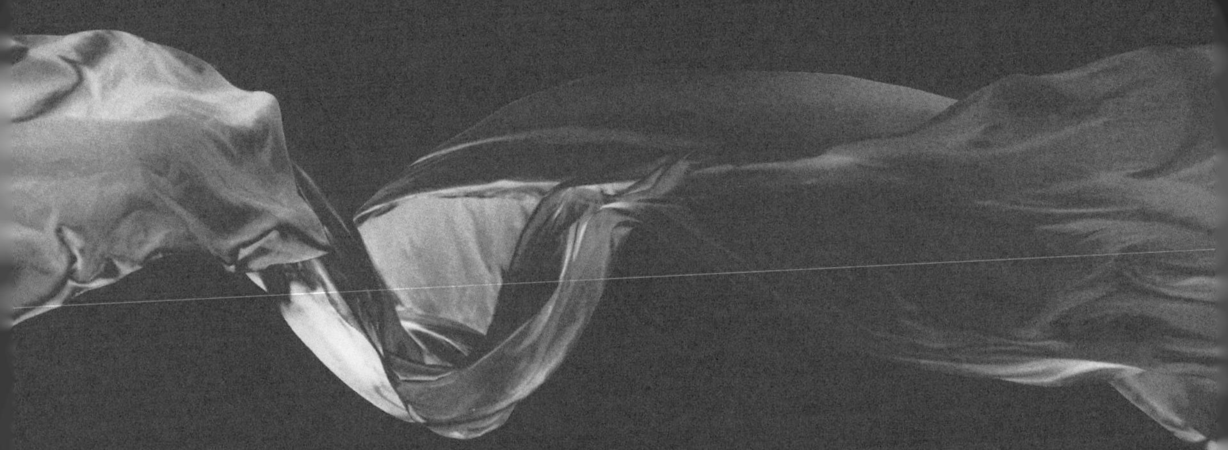

SESSION FIVE

GROUP GETTING STARTED: (10-15 minutes)

SESSION FIVE: THE WONDER OF FRIENDSHIPS

HOMEWORK GROUP DISCUSSION

1 Ask participants to share three moments they recorded in the Wonderstruck Journal in which they encountered the wonder of God and His handiwork this week. In what ways is the process of recording these moments helping you to recognize more of them?

2 From Day One's homework, what have you found really works for you in methods, techniques, or approaches when it comes to prayer?

3 From the homework in Days Two, Three, and Four that examined nine different prayers of Jesus, what challenged you most about Jesus' prayer life?

4 Reflecting on the final day's homework, how can the other members of the group persevere in prayer alongside you?

EXPERIENTIAL ACTIVITY: HAVE A BALL WITH FRIENDS

WHAT YOU'LL NEED:

- A beach ball
- A permanent marker

1 Write questions about friendship all over the ball. They may include:

- **What are three words that describe your best friend?**
- **What's the most important quality in a friend?**
- **What's your favorite thing to do with your friends?**
- **What nicknames do you have for your friends?**
- **Whose friendship in the Bible do you admire most?**
- **What is one character quality you need to improve to be a better friend?**
- **What's one character quality you possess that makes you a good friend?**

Vary the questions until the ball is covered.

2 Ask participants to stand in a circle and begin by tossing the ball to someone.

3 The person who catches the ball must answer whatever question his or her left thumb touches while catching the ball.

4 Continue tossing the ball for five to ten minutes or until everyone has answered at least one of the questions.

PLAY THE SESSION FIVE VIDEO: [21:45]

NOTES

VIDEO DISCUSSION

1 List three of the wondrous rewards of a healthy, vibrant friendship you've experienced in your life. (Examples: knowing you're not alone, being loved just as you are, being challenged in your relationship with God, etc.)

2 Ask someone to read Proverbs 27:17 aloud. When have you experienced this passage being true in one of your friendships? Who are some of your "iron" friends?

3 Reflecting on the Five Levels of Communication that Margaret described, which level of communication do you tend to use in your most satisfying, vibrant relationships? Explain.

4 When have you struggled to adjust your expectations of what the other person should bring to the friendship? What did you learn about God, yourself, and the other person through this experience?

5 Ask someone to read Ephesians 4:29-32 aloud. What is one difficult conversation you've been putting off? How can you adhere to this passage as you have the conversation? Urge members to pray for one another as they commit to having the difficult conversation this week in order to strengthen a relationship and make it more healthy and vibrant.

6 In what ways have you sensed God inviting you into a deeper, more intimate friendship with Him in this season of your life? How have you responded?

CLOSING PRAYER

As you close in prayer ask:

- that each person's heart, mind, and life awaken to a greater sense of God's wonder
- God to open each participant's eyes to the wonder of friendship in their lives
- the Holy Spirit to give participants the strength and courage to strengthen their friendships with others.

DAY ONE

NO LONGER AT ARMS LENGTH

WHEN LEIF AND I LEFT ALASKA for Colorado, we knew the time to start a new life in a new place had arrived. We began in our neighborhood, but many of the "hey neighbor" conversations never moved beyond surfacy and shallow. We reached out to those from the church, but none of our invitations were reciprocated.

THIS WEEK:

If you are following along in the trade book, read chapter ".007: Magic in the Table," and tackle the five days of homework to prepare for the next gathering.

When have you felt the pain of unrequited friendships?

I love having friends. I bet you do, too! Few things are more delightful than kicking off my shoes and spending an afternoon drinking iced tea with someone with whom I can most fully be myself, knowing we're both rooting for each other to become everything God intended.

For me, the wonder of friendship is found in the tender moments that can easily pass by without noticing:

- Those moments a friend says the exact words I needed to hear.
- Those instances when a friend lets me process aloud without judgment.
- The invitation of a friend to do something I wouldn't do on my own—but the gentle prodding expands my imagination of what's possible.
- Those times I'm reminded that no matter what I'm facing, I'm not alone.

BONUS ACTIVITY:

Spend time committing Colossians 3:12-14 to memory this week. You'll find a flash card on page 177.

What are some of the wonders of friendship you've experienced? Add your responses to the Wonderstruck Journal.

Yet making new friends takes time, energy, and effort. Over the years I've moved around—living in Florida, North Carolina, Colorado, and even Alaska—and each time I've had to make new friends. But I've also experienced times in life when I wasn't the one moving. Instead, the people I knew and loved, one by one, moved away, and I had to start from ground zero to build new friendships again.

Make a list of the moments in your life when you've had to start over building new friendships. Which were the most challenging? The easiest? What made the difference?

One of the keys to developing healthy, vibrant relationships is recognizing that making friends takes time. That's why choosing wisely whom we're going to build a relationship with is so important. Proverbs 12:26 tells us, "The righteous choose their friends carefully." We need to be intentional about praying for discernment as we develop our relationships and trust that God is going to bring people into our lives as gifts—people whom we can both love and be loved by.

What does Proverbs 13:20 reveal about the effects friendships can have on you?

+ BONUS ACTIVITY:

A great resource on rediscovering the art of neighboring that has challenged me in my own faith journey is *www.artofneighboring.com*.

On the continuum below, mark how often you find yourself in the companion of the wise.

I find myself the companion of the wise often.	I never find myself the companion of the wise.

When have you found yourself to be the companion of the wise? How did they affect your relationship with God?

When have you found yourself to be the companion of fools? How did they affect your relationship with God?

A few years ago, I developed a friendship with someone I had a blast with every time we were together. I loved spending time with her, but I soon discovered she was making some unwise choices in her life—and her foolish behavior was creating new temptations for me. I found myself sliding into gossip and slander. I was tempted to cut corners and become less honest when I was around her. I soon found dissatisfaction popping up in my life and relationships that I'd never experienced before. Instead of challenging me to become more Christlike, I was being drawn away through my relationship with her. I had to take a step back.

Sometimes knowing when to pull back from a friendship is hard—especially when we're trying to make a difference in that person's life—but we need to ask ourselves: Are we more of an influence toward godliness or are we being influenced for ungodliness? Whenever the primary influence is that you're being drawn away from God, the time has come to take a step back and prayerfully reassess.

What does 1 Corinthians 15:33 reveal about the dangers friendships carry with them?

What three things do you think we should look for in identifying the good company we need to keep?

-
-
-

Do you need to make any changes in your selection of friends right now? If so, what is stopping you from making them?

One of the biggest lessons I learned in our most recent move about developing healthy, vibrant friendships is that, even though I was inviting people into our home, I wasn't really inviting them into my life. I was holding them at arm's length. I'd share details about my life but nothing too personal. I'd change the subject whenever the discussion became too intimate. I'd stick to shallow, neutral topics. And I'd disappear into the kitchen and away from the conversation whenever anything became too involved. At a certain point, I realized that if acquaintances were going to blossom into friendships, I needed to let people into my life.

Have you ever used unhealthy tactics to hold people at arm's length? If so, what behaviors can you identify that you've used?

I find comfort in knowing I'm not the only one who struggled with holding people at arm's length. Tucked into the Book of Ruth is the story of a family whose lives are marked by loss. A woman named Naomi is married to Elimelek and has two sons, Mahlon and Kilion. Each son marries a Moabite woman—one named Orpah and the

QUOTABLE:

The temptation to live a guarded life allures everyone, but any walls constructed for protection only lead to isolation. Receiving the life God has for you requires vulnerability.

NOTABLE:

Orpah's name is Moabite meaning "the back of the neck," possibly foreshadowing that she turned her back on Naomi. Ruth's name means "friend, companion," something she demonstrated by remaining with her mother-in-law.

other Ruth. Naomi's husband and two sons die, and she is left with no one. She encourages her daughters-in-law, Orpah and Ruth, to return to their homeland.

Both women protest that they'll stay with Naomi. But again, Naomi persists that they should return home and find new husbands. In essence, she throws up her hands and says, "No, this isn't best for you so you should stay away."

How does Orpah's response to Naomi in Ruth 1:14 differ from Ruth's response?

Afterward, Naomi encourages Ruth to go with her sister-in-law. In response, Ruth delivers some of the most famous words of Scripture:

What does Ruth's plea in Ruth 1:15-18 reveal about her determination to stay with Naomi?

Though Naomi tries to throw her arms up and say, "Don't follow me!" and "Don't get too close right now," Ruth refuses to listen. In the process, she makes herself more vulnerable to Naomi and Naomi becomes even more vulnerable to Ruth. Their friendship and relationship grows deeper. Together they travel to Bethlehem and arrive just as the barley harvest begins, where a divine series of events lead them to safety, provision, and an unforgettable love story.

Much like Naomi, by my response and interactions I had been telling people not to get too close. And like Naomi, I came to a place where I realized I had to let people into my life—even with all my imperfections and weaknesses. I decided to become more honest in my conversations and also to reach out to specific people and ask them to pray with me. Through prayer and risking vulnerability, I found myself in healthier, more vibrant relationships.

When are you most tempted to hold people at arm's length?

QUOTABLE:

"Don't urge me to leave you or to turn back from you. Where you go I will go, and where you stay I will stay. Your people will be my people and your God my God." –Ruth 1:16

How does holding people at arm's length short-circuit the incredible gift of friendship God has for you?

Identify two people you know who might have a deeper friendship with you if you were willing to be more vulnerable.

Send an e-mail or text and invite them to get together over the upcoming week. While you're together, be intentional about asking questions and sharing from your life. Make time to pray together.

Most of the healthy, vibrant, and long-lasting friendships in our lives will take longer than we think to develop, but they're well worth the time and the risk of vulnerability. Friendships require investment, but, as we'll discover in tomorrow's homework, they can pay dividends for a lifetime.

CLOSING PRAYER: Spend some time making a list of friends who are currently in your life. As you pray for each person, ask God what you can do to strengthen the friendship and become a better friend to that person.

DAY TWO

WISDOM AND FRIENDSHIPS

LEARNING HOW TO DEVELOP HEALTHY, vibrant friendships doesn't happen overnight, but takes years—and a whole lot of practice. Along the way, we'll all make mistakes, learn to extend grace, and hopefully become better friends to others.

I recently reached out to my friends on Facebook asking what lessons they've learned over the years for nurturing healthy, vibrant relationships. I want to share some of what they've discovered.

As you read these statements about friendship, underline (or write in the margin) the key ideas you could use to help you build better friendships.

Mark the one you struggle with the most to put into practice in your friendships. Why do you think you struggle with it?

- ☐ **"Healthy friendships always encourage and expect you to grow—to become who you were created and called to be—without agenda or hope for personal gain." –Ellis**

- ☐ **"I've learned that kindness and grace are really important to lasting friendships. When they are priorities, it's easier to know when to speak and when to be silent, when to listen more, and when someone needs affirmation. Grace paves the way for forgiveness and gentleness. I'm so thankful to God for the precious friends in my life!" –Terri**

- ☐ **"I've learned that healthy friendships are found with those of us who accept each other's imperfections." –Jeffrey**

- ☐ **"You don't have to be everyone's friend. And keep cherishing those life-longers with whom you've traveled far." –Jennifer**

I've found all the responses listed above to be powerful reminders of the things that I'm constantly learning about being a better friend. Good friends love me as I am, but they also love me enough not to leave me there. Good friends not only exhibit kindness and grace but challenge me to grow in faith as well. Good friends are worth keeping for a lifetime.

One friendship I've always admired in the Bible is the special relationship between Paul and Timothy. As an older believer, Paul served as a mentor to Timothy in ministry and life. Paul was a steady voice of encouragement and wisdom as Timothy prepared to handle the church in Ephesus. But friendships aren't one-way. Imagine the joy Paul felt in the friendship he developed with Timothy. Consider the delight Paul experienced in sharing his faith in a tangible way by investing in Timothy.

What does 1 Timothy 1:1-2,18 and 2 Timothy 1:1-8 reveal about the friendship that developed between Paul and Timothy?

Who in your life has been a Paul to you—encouraging you to grow into the fullness of being a follower of Jesus Christ?

Who in your own life are you being a Paul to—encouraging them to grow into the fullness of being a follower of Jesus Christ?

If you don't have a Paul or Timothy in your life right now, who can you begin reaching out to in your community, workplace, or church to begin developing these kinds of friendships?

NOTABLE:

Paul and Timothy met in Lystra as described in Acts 16:1. Timothy grew up with a Jewish mother and Gentile father.

QUOTABLE:

"You, however, know all about my teaching, my way of life, my purpose, faith, patience, love, endurance, persecutions, sufferings—what kinds of things happened to me in Antioch, Iconium and Lystra, the persecutions I endured. Yet the Lord rescued me from all of them." –2 Timothy 3:10-11

BONUS ACTIVITY:

I'd love to hear your wisdom on developing a healthy, vibrant friendship. Post your response to this question on my Facebook page at *www.facebook.com/margaretfeinberg.*

As we develop healthy, vibrant friendships, we'll continue learning more lessons. Consider some more of the wisdom my friends on Facebook shared:

"I went through a temperament awareness course and learned that people, family, and friends don't necessarily do things to bug you; they are just wired that way and God made them that way. Understanding the different temperaments and interaction styles people have gave me greater understanding and appreciation for the similarities and differences we all have and share. Communication is much better and my friendships have been even healthier now that I understand them better." –Monica

"I actually learned about healthy friendships with a group of women we would meet with for Bible study. I learned that you really can have healthy friendships with more than just one person at a time. These women have helped me learn about my marriage, my faith, and myself. We laugh and cry together and can count on (each other's) support at all times." –Elizabeth

What would you add to the list of lessons learned about developing healthy, vibrant relationships?

For me, one of the most meaningful came from my friend, Deanna:

"Friends are gifts in this life, but they can't (and shouldn't) fulfill all our needs. Only Jesus can. Not sure how I learned it, but I'm pretty sure I need to relearn it often." –Deanna

Like Deanna, I've had to relearn the lesson that no single friend or large group of friends can meet all my needs. The role is reserved for God alone. When I forget this foundational truth, my friendships suffer as I place more of a burden on them than they were meant to bear. All too easily, I can slip into thinking that others can meet my needs, make me feel better, and say the perfect words instead of turning to God.

Yet throughout the Scripture we're reminded that God is the only One in our lives who will not leave us, nor forsake us. God is the best friend we'll ever have and He extends the invitation of friendship with Him to us each and every day.

What do Deuteronomy 7:9 and Psalm 89:2 reveal to you about God's faithfulness?

When in the last six months has God shown Himself faithful to you?

Many years ago, I remember being in a season of life when I struggled in every direction—relationally, financially, and professionally. A friend handed me a passage of Scripture on a crumpled up piece of paper. She said this particular passage had been a voice of encouragement in her life and she hoped it would be one in mine, too. I never imagined a wrinkled, handwritten piece of paper could have such an impact on my life. Every time I read the words, they anchor me in the reality of God's love and His desire for a relationship with me.

NOTABLE:

Paul sends Timothy two pastoral letters. First Timothy addresses false teaching. Second Timothy encourages Timothy and other believers in the faith.

In the space below, write down any particularly meaningful phrases or words from Isaiah 43:1-7.

As you reflect on Isaiah 43:1-7 over the next few days, I pray you'll walk in the truth that you are loved fully, just as you are, by the Creator of the stars that shoot across the sky and the spiky, furry animals that creep across the earth. Being rooted in this truth will allow friendships to develop and strengthen. Join me over the next few days as we continue to dive into how to develop healthy friendships.

CLOSING PRAYER: Spend some time prayerfully considering who in your life—family, friends, coworkers—you've been looking to fill a need or a place in your heart that God longs to fill. Ask God to reveal any areas in your life where He wants you to become more dependent on Him.

DAY THREE

GUARDING YOUR WONDROUS FRIENDSHIPS

IT'S AMAZING HOW QUICKLY our friendships can go awry because of misunderstanding and miscommunication. Whenever we assume the worst of someone else, our relationships unravel, the friendship cools, and the close connection is lost.

In order to experience the wonder of friendship, we need to guard our relationships. Just as the Bible provides insight on how to nurture healthy, vibrant friendships, the Scripture also offers warnings on what can ruin a friendship.

Reflecting on Proverbs 16:28, when have you experienced gossip undermining your friendships?

One of the biggest enemies of friendship is gossip. In some ways this is the most challenging, because gossip can create a false sense of intimacy and connection. Often, when someone shares the juicy details of someone's private life or you've-gotta-hear-this news, leaning in to hear what they have to say is easy. But their words are often anything but encouraging or edifying.

Anyone who gossips to you will also gossip about you—this is no secret. Gossip has a way of building the gossiper up because of their knowledge, which feeds pride, arrogance, and a false sense of worth. Gossip also tends to highlight faults and failings and reveal embarrassing details about someone else. If left unchecked, gossip can undermine even the strongest of friendships.

How can you place Proverbs 11:12-13 and Proverbs 21:23 into action in your life?

3 TIPS TO SHORT-CIRCUITING GOSSIP

1 **YOU DON'T HAVE TO PARTICIPATE IN GOSSIP.** You can choose to hold your tongue and try to shift the topic of conversation. If appropriate, quietly remove yourself from the conversation.

2 **FOCUS ON THE GOOD, TRUE, AND BEAUTIFUL.** If someone is the topic of gossip, choose to comment on the person's strengths, contributions, or highlight a positive difference this person has made in your life.

3 **GENTLY APPLY THE GOLDEN RULE.** With a kind and even lighthearted tone, you can gently remind those talking that you wouldn't want someone talking about you this way and ask to change the topic.

What would you add as a fourth tip on how to short-circuit gossip?

NOTABLE:

Discover examples of biblical friendships: Jonathan and David (1 Samuel 18–20), Elijah and Elisha (1 Kings 19 and 2 Kings 2), Jesus and Peter (John 21), Paul and Barnabas (Acts 9:26-30).

In addition to guarding our friendships from gossip, we also need to protect them from unforgiveness. Whenever unforgiveness enters a friendship, the relationship soon deteriorates. Unforgiveness is like a snare that tears people apart. Proverbs 17:9 reminds us, "Love prospers when a fault is forgiven, but dwelling on it separates close friends" (NLT). Jesus challenges His followers repeatedly to forgive and keep on forgiving.

Reflecting on Matthew 18:21-35, what situation with a friend has been the most challenging to forgive?

How does focusing on how much God has forgiven you strengthen your resolve to forgive others?

On the continuum below, mark whether you find forgiving others or asking for forgiveness easier.

I forgive others easily. —————————— I can ask for forgiveness easily.

NOTABLE:

Don't miss Session Six: The Wonder of Forgiveness, where we'll dive more deeply into what extending and receiving forgiveness means.

Who in your life do you need to ask forgiveness from right now?

We must also guard our friendships from selfishness. I'm always amazed at how easily selfishness can slip into my friendships and the subtle forms it takes. If left unchecked, I end up squeezing friends into my schedule when most convenient for me and squeezing the life out of them as I decide where we should eat and what we should do—without even consulting them!

Every good friendship requires give and take—and this means much more give than take. Becoming a good friend means being ready to give, serve, and sacrifice. Sometimes being a good friend means eating at a restaurant you don't like and watching a movie you'd rather not see, all to show love and appreciation for someone else. I recently went to a movie I didn't want to see with a friend I adored. When we walked out of the theater, I still didn't like the film, but I adored my friend even more. And she knew it.

When we place ourselves above others and focus on only our concerns, selfishness runs rampant in our lives—and other sins and self-destructive behaviors soon follow.

Reflecting on James 3:14-18, how have you allowed selfishness to undermine your friendships? What have you learned from the experience?

Which of the two women in 1 Kings 3:16-27 is the more selfish? Reflecting on this story, what is the fruit of selfishness?

In what friendships do you need to walk in humility and grace by placing others before yourself?

Our friendships provide opportunities to grow in Christlikeness at every turn. Don't miss your opportunity to grow.

CLOSING PRAYER: Spend some time praying for each of your friends. As you lift each person's name up to God, ask if there's anything you need to do or consider in order to both protect and strengthen the friendship and make it more glorifying to God.

QUOTABLE:

"To love at all is to be vulnerable. Love anything and your heart will certainly be wrung and possibly broken. If you want to make sure of keeping it intact, you must give your heart to no one, not even to an animal. Wrap it carefully round with hobbies and little luxuries; avoid all entanglements; lock it up safe in the casket or coffin of your selfishness. But in that casket—safe, dark, motionless, airless—it will change. It will not be broken; it will become unbreakable, impenetrable, irredeemable. The alternative to tragedy, or at least to the risk of tragedy, is damnation. The only place outside Heaven where you can be perfectly safe from all the dangers and perturbations of love is Hell." –C.S. Lewis, author and theologian[14]

DAY FOUR

THE DIFFICULT CONVERSATIONS

WHEN DEVELOPING THRIVING, long-lasting friendships, sooner or later we have to engage in The Difficult Conversation (TDC). We may need to say something or raise an issue to bring out the best in the other person or to make the relationship more enjoyable and healthy.

A while back a friend had to have a difficult conversation with me. We spent time together regularly taking walks, sharing meals, and enjoying each other's company. One day she announced she had something that she needed to talk about. We began by affirming our friendship and the importance of the relationship in her life. Then she shared she had noticed an unhealthy pattern in our friendship. She said while I asked lots of questions of her and she shared freely, I seemed reserved and unwilling to share from my life. She said she wanted me to know so the relationship could grow stronger.

QUOTABLE:

"Like a bee, a word may have honey in its sting." –Jewish Proverb

In the moment, the words felt like a bee sting.

How did you feel the last time someone had a difficult conversation with you? What did you learn from the experience?

"Thank you for telling me," I said, a bit off-balance from her words. My mind raced through our conversations during the last few times we'd hung out together. She was right! I hadn't been sharing freely or openly, but as I thought about the reason why I had to make a confession to her.

"One of the reasons I don't share from my life is because you never ask anything about me—even how I'm doing," I said.

We both sat in a thick silence as we realized the unhealthy pattern in our relationship.

"I'll start being more intentional about asking you questions," she replied.

"And I promise to take the initiative and share even when you're not asking a question," I said.

From that day our relationship grew stronger than it had ever been before, and I'm so grateful she took the initiative to have TDC.

When was the last time you had TDC with someone and it went well?

When was the last time you had TDC with someone and it didn't go as well?

QUOTABLE:

"Listen to advice and accept discipline, and at the end you will be counted among the wise." —Proverbs 19:20

What do you think might have made the difference?

One of the reasons the conversation went so well was because of my friend's approach. She began by affirming our friendship and the importance of it in her life. This established an understanding that in whatever she was going to say next—she was not only rooting for me but for us as friends. Then, she clearly identified the unhealthy pattern without using accusations, but rather undergirding her words and tone with grace and love.

How have you found Proverbs 27:6 to be true in your own life?

What wisdom do you find in Colossians 3:12-14 regarding your approach and tone to having The Difficult Conversation with someone?

9 TIPS TO MAKE TDC EASIER

1 PRAY. Spend time specifically praying for the person you're going to approach. Ask God for wisdom on the best way to raise the topic as well as the timing.

2 WRAP YOUR MIND AND HEART IN SCRIPTURE. Spend time reflecting on passages such as 1 Corinthians 13 and invite the Holy Spirit to reshape your attitude, tone, and approach through God's Word.

3 DON'T WAIT. After you've prayed and studied the Scripture, pick a day soon that you can meet with the person. All too often, delaying the conversation only makes matters worse.

4 PAY ATTENTION TO BODY POSTURE AND TONE. Establish eye contact. Sitting for the conversation is preferable because it's a less aggressive posture. Make sure your arms aren't crossed, which can communicate closed-mindedness. Use a gentle, kind, and warm tone.

5 AFFIRM THE PERSON. Begin by affirming the person and their importance in your life.

6 BE SPECIFIC AND BRIEF ABOUT THE CONCERN. If you tell someone they're forgetful, identify specific moments—with dates and times—they've forgotten something particularly meaningful to you and how this made you feel. Otherwise, your words are too broad and general to be helpful. Avoid accusatory tone or language. Use words such as "I feel" instead of "You always."

7 MOVE TO A COLLABORATIVE SOLUTION QUICKLY. After you identify the concern, reaffirm the importance of the person and their friendship. Reiterate your desire to move beyond this concern. This will transition the conversation from "you versus them" to both of you collaborating against a problem. If appropriate, offer a potential solution.

8 LISTEN TO THE OTHER PERSON. After you bring up an issue, sometimes the other person will reveal a misunderstanding that may indicate you need to change your mind or apologize. Be prepared to see the issue from a different perspective and make changes in your life.

9 REAFFIRM THE PROGRESS MADE THROUGH THE CONVERSATION. Thank the person for his or her time and willingness to discuss the issue. If appropriate, pray together. Then, reaffirm the person and the important role he or she plays in your life.

What would you add as another tip to make The Difficult Conversation easier?

QUOTABLE:

"Make every effort to keep the unity of the Spirit through the bond of peace." –Ephesians 4:3

What are three difficult conversations in your family, workplace, or community that you've been putting off having?

-
-
-

How does 1 Corinthians 13 prepare you to approach these difficult conversations?

BONUS ACTIVITY:

Having TDC isn't easy. I'd love to pray for you as you begin this process. E-mail your prayer requests to *wonderstruck@ margaretfeinberg.com.*

What practical steps can you take to schedule these difficult conversations in the next week?

Prepare to discuss at least one of the things you've learned through having The Difficult Conversation with the group next time you meet.

CLOSING PRAYER: Spend some time asking God for the grace, strength, and love to engage in The Difficult Conversation with someone in order to strengthen the relationship.

DAY FIVE

THE INVITATION TO BECOME MORE CHRISTLIKE

IF YOU LOOK IN THE CLOSET near the front door of our house, you'll find loads of shoes. But if you look closely, you'll notice that some of the pairs of shoes aren't the right size for Leif or me. Why do I have shoes in my closet that don't fit?

Because I have a dear friend named Carol. We've spent so many evenings taking walks together after work that she actually stores her shoes—and even a change of clothes—at our house. I've known Carol for more than 15 years and I treasure her friendship. And even though she lives in another state now, she still keeps several pairs of shoes in our closet.

When I think back over the years of our friendship, I'm amazed at how much she's challenged me to become more Christlike. Sometimes that happened through having The Difficult Conversation with each other—always seasoned with grace and love. Sometimes that occurred because she challenged me with a word of truth or hope at just the perfect time. And sometimes that took place because I caught a glimpse of God at work in her life.

BONUS ACTIVITY:

Celebrate friendship this week. Invite a friend on a walk around the nearest lake, go to the shooting range, or spend time at your favorite sushi restaurant. Take time to recognize and celebrate friendships in your life.

Carol has told countless stories over the years of sharing her faith that have made me want to be bolder in sharing mine. She's taught me about overcoming through Christ, despite the many obstacles faced. She's shown me love on my most unlovable days—and they're pretty impressive! She's prayed for me, expressed kindness in a billion different moments, and brought a word of peace when life's storms seemed too much to bear. But one of the most powerful things she's given me is the gift of her presence—simply being with me year after year as a friend.

That's why whenever I see her shoes in our closet I smile.

Good friends challenge us to develop more of the character of Christ in our lives—and they often do it by simply being themselves. Created in the image of God, they reveal facets of the nature of God and give us opportunities to become more Christlike. At times, they encourage us to hold onto our faith when we need it most.

When the topic comes to friends who have been through the fire together, I can't help but think of Shadrach, Meshach, and Abednego. They stood unified in their resolve to face the fiery furnace rather than give into the king's decree.

Reflecting on Daniel 3:1-30, how do you think the story might have ended differently if these three men hadn't stood together in their faith and friendship?

QUOTABLE:

"Greater love has no one than this: to lay down one's life for one's friends."–John 15:13

Who has stood alongside you through a fiery ordeal in life? How did those people strengthen your faith because of their presence?

Jesus is the ultimate example of a true friend. He laid down His life for His friends. Through our friendships we have the opportunity to grow in Christlikeness.

What does Romans 5:7-8 reveal about God's love for us?

Which of your current friendships are inviting you to a greater level of self-sacrifice in order to demonstrate God's love?

Have you pulled back from any friendships because you're unwilling to demonstrate a greater level of self-sacrifice? If so, what has been the result?

QUOTABLE:

"My best friend is the one who brings out the best in me." –Henry Ford, American industrialist

Over the years, I've noticed that all of the friends in my life have something to teach me about Christ. Some of my friends remind me of the importance and strength found in joy. Others have an ability to remain cool-headed and exude God's peace in the toughest of times. And still others knock my socks off with their kindness to everyone in every situation.

In the space below, make a list of the fruit of the Spirit mentioned in Galatians 5:22-23.

Next to each item listed above, write the name of someone you know who has challenged or encouraged you to grow in that area because of their friendship with you. Send a note or e-mail letting them know the difference they've made in your life.

Don't wait to celebrate the wonder of friendship. Pick up the phone. Text a message. Schedule a time together just to catch up, share, laugh, pray, and play together.

I hope you'll join us for the presentation and discussion next week as we dive into the wonder of forgiveness. Not only are we freely forgiven, we're called to spill that forgiveness onto others. This is a session you're not going to want to miss!

CLOSING PRAYER: Spend some time thanking God for the friends He has brought into your life. Ask Him to expand your heart to others in the weeks ahead.

THE WONDER OF FORGIVENESS

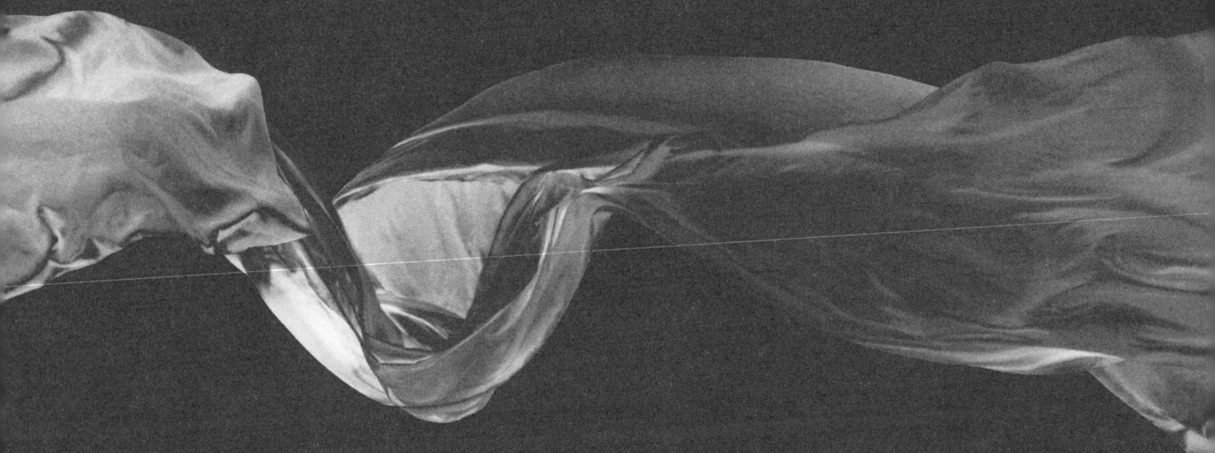

SESSION SIX

GROUP GETTING STARTED: (10-15 minutes)

SESSION SIX:
THE WONDER OF FORGIVENESS

HOMEWORK GROUP DISCUSSION

1 Ask participants to share three moments they recorded in the Wonderstruck Journal in which they encountered the wonder of God and His handiwork this week.

2 Day One's homework challenged you with the question, "How does holding people at arm's length short-circuit the incredible gift of friendship God has for you?" How did you respond? Who did you identify as two people you could have deeper friendships with if you were willing to be more vulnerable? Did you reach out to them? Why or why not?

3 The homework from Day Two offered tips for growing healthy relationships. In addition to the ideas offered in this lesson, what is the greatest piece of wisdom you've discovered in learning to develop vibrant, healthy relationships in your life?

4 Day Four's homework challenged you to have The Difficult Conversation (TDC) with at least one person in your life this week. Share with the group your experience and what you learned.

EXPERIENTIAL ACTIVITY: LEARNING TO FORGIVE

WHAT YOU'LL NEED:

- Small pieces of paper
- A pen
- A bowl

1 Before gathering, on each piece of paper write one positive "I" statement about forgiveness and place them in a bowl. Here are some suggestions:

- I forgive easily.
- I never replay moments of hurt, pain, or loss in my mind.
- Whenever I forgive, I immediately forget.
- Forgiveness is as natural to me as breathing.

2 Ask participants to draw one piece of paper from the bowl. Then tell them that if the statement is absolutely true of them they should stand against one wall in the room. If the statement is absolutely not true of them then they should stand against the opposite wall. If the statement is somewhat true of them then they should stand somewhere in the middle according to whether the statement is more or less true of them.

3 As they're standing, invite participants to share what their strip of paper says and why they chose to stand in that spot.

4 Discuss the following questions:

Why do you think forgiving others is challenging?

What does forgiving someone versus not forgiving someone cost you?

When have you believed you forgave someone but soon realized you didn't?

What attitudes, responses, or characteristics tend to expose an area of unforgiveness?

PLAY THE SESSION SIX VIDEO: [19:30]

NOTES

VIDEO DISCUSSION

1 What kinds of offenses do you find the hardest to forgive?

2 Who is the person you've struggled to forgive most?

3 When have you delayed forgiving someone and discovered that the slow response affected your ability to forgive?

4 What consequences of unforgiveness have you experienced in your life?

5 How do you break the cycle of replaying someone's offense in your mind repeatedly?

CLOSING PRAYER

As you close in prayer ask:

- that each person's heart, mind, and life awaken to a greater sense of God's wonder
- God to reveal areas in our hearts where we're harboring unforgiveness
- the Holy Spirit to give us the grace and strength to walk as those who are wholly forgiven and free to forgive others.

DAY ONE

REMEMBER HOW AND WHEN GOD HAS FORGIVEN YOU

THIS WEEK:

If you're following along in the trade book, read chapters ".008: The Disappearing Silver Necklace," ".009: Miracle on the Runway," and ".010: The Legend of Cactus Jack" and tackle the five days of homework to prepare for the next gathering.

BONUS ACTIVITY:

Spend time committing Micah 7:18-19 to memory this week. You'll find a flash card on page 177.

NOTABLE:

Eugene Davidson is not the man's real name. In considering an alternative, I confess to being tempted to call him "Boil" or some other name that carried a double meaning. But I chose to call him Eugene, because it's reminiscent of the Greek word "eulogeo" meaning "blessing" and "David" meaning "beloved." Luke 6:28 challenges us to bless those who curse us, and in this case, I decided to follow the words of Jesus literally.

WHEN I FOUND OUT Eugene Davidson's company had embezzled us, I was confused, bewildered, angry, and upset. In the months that followed, I pieced together the details of how we'd been duped and robbed. Yet despite the loss and stress of the experience, I knew I needed to forgive Eugene Davidson—a man who I'd never met and am unlikely to ever meet. The journey of forgiveness challenged me in my faith and pushed me to understand God's grace even greater.

Sometimes we have misperceptions about forgiveness that skew the deeper work God wants to do in our lives. Here are five truths about forgiveness.

As you read, mark the ones you've wrestled with or discovered to be true in your life:

- ☐ **Forgiveness is not only about saying I forgive you. If you were forced as a child to say sorry, you know that forgiveness requires more than just a verbal acknowledgement.**
- ☐ **Forgiveness isn't accompanied by a list of requirements. True forgiveness isn't dependent on the other person's response or actions and cannot be earned.**
- ☐ **Forgiveness is not a pass to become a doormat. Choosing to forgive does not mean you need to sign up for the same mistreatment a second time. You can forgive someone without having to submit to the same hurtful behavior again.**
- ☐ **Forgiveness is not denying the wrong took place. Sometimes we're so quick to forget an offense we never acknowledge the depth of the wounding that took place. Real forgiveness doesn't deny the truth but deals with it head on.**
- ☐ **Forgiveness is not a guarantee for reconciliation. Some people paint the picture that if you forgive, everything will turn out**

rosy for everyone. Sometimes this is simply not possible, but we are still called to forgive.

The forgiveness God calls us to is much deeper and more robust.

As you read the following definitions underline any words that stand out to you:

FORGIVE:
1. TO EXCUSE FOR A FAULT OR AN OFFENSE; PARDON.
2. TO RENOUNCE ANGER OR RESENTMENT AGAINST.
3. TO ABSOLVE FROM PAYMENT OF (A DEBT, FOR EXAMPLE).[15]

Which of the three definitions of forgiveness is most challenging to you? Why?

QUOTABLE:

"For if you forgive other people when they sin against you, your heavenly Father will also forgive you. But if you do not forgive others their sins, your Father will not forgive your sins." –Matthew 6:14-15

For me, the second definition is one of the biggest challenges. Though in my mind, I may be able to choose forgiveness, sometimes my emotions take a while to catch up. I can say, "I forgive you" with my lips long before I feel those words in my heart. Yet the Bible encourages us not merely to forgive, but to forgive quickly.

Reflecting on Ephesians 4:31-32, how ready are you to forgive a wrong in your everyday life? On the continuum below, mark your answer:

I need a lot of time to forgive a wrong. — I'm immediately ready to forgive a wrong.

One of the great wonders of forgiveness is its multifaceted nature. Forgiveness isn't only something we receive for ourselves. Forgiveness sets us free from those who have wronged us and those whom we have wronged. Like a stream, forgiveness is meant to flow through us, refreshing others along the way.

Jesus said that one of the primary ways people would recognize His disciples was by their love for one another (John 13:35). Through forgiveness, we demonstrate the power of Christ's love for others to see.

When have you seen a person forgive someone else that was particularly powerful or meaningful to you?

QUOTABLE:

"'In your anger do not sin': Do not let the sun go down while you are still angry, and do not give the devil a foothold." –Ephesians 4:26-27

Despite the clear call of God to forgive others, sometimes it's messy, difficult, and feels impossible. At times, our efforts and expressions of forgiveness may not go as well as we had hoped.

Why do you think Jesus says that God blesses those who are treated badly for doing right immediately after He blesses those who make peace in Matthew 5:9-10?

When have you tried to express forgiveness for someone or ask forgiveness of someone and it didn't go as well as you had hoped?

NOTABLE:

The first servant owes the king 10,000 talents—an immeasurable amount because a talent wasn't a coin, but a unit of money. Modern scholars equivocate this to more than two and a half billion dollars in today's terms. The second servant owes the first servant 100 denarii, which is equivalent to around $4,000.

In the moments when we struggle to forgive someone else, remembering how much God has forgiven us is important.

In His fourth discourse recorded in Matthew, Jesus tells a parable that illustrates a man who forgot how much he'd been forgiven. Jesus reminds believers that we aren't only supposed to speak the gospel, but actually live it out through humility, reconciliation, forgiveness, and love.

Why do you think the servant in Matthew 18:21-35 was so unforgiving?

When do situations or people tend to cause you to become unforgiving?

One of the reasons for the servant's lack of forgiveness is because he forgot the great debt he had been forgiven. Like the servant, we, too, can lose sight of how much God has forgiven us. Every so often we need to pause and reflect on how much we've been forgiven. That's why the focus of this lesson is on the following activity. I'd like you to take time and create a list of some of the things for which God has forgiven you. Your entries may come from the past few days or over the course of your lifetime. Don't rush as you fill in the chart. Ask the Holy Spirit to bring significant moments to mind.

NOTABLE:

Jesus' parable in Matthew 18 begins the same as the other parables of the mysteries of heaven found in Matthew 13.

In the space provided, record at least 30 different things for which God has forgiven you:

1.

2.

3.

4.

5.

6.

7.

8.

9.

10.

11.

12.

13.

QUOTABLE:

"We are to forgive so that we may enjoy God's goodness without feeling the weight of anger burning deep within our hearts. Forgiveness does not mean we recant the fact that what happened to us was wrong. Instead, we roll our burdens onto the Lord and allow Him to carry them for us." –Charles Stanley, author and pastor[16]

14.

15.

16.

17.

18.

19.

20.

21.

22.

23.

24.

25.

26.

27.

28.

29.

30.

QUOTABLE:

"Who is a God like you, who pardons sin and forgives the transgression of the remnant of his inheritance? You do not stay angry forever but delight to show mercy. You will again have compassion on us; you will tread our sins underfoot and hurl all our iniquities into the depths of the sea." —Micah 7:18-19

Does anything on the list stand out as particularly meaningful? If so, why? How does reflecting on God's forgiveness strengthen your resolve to forgive others?

Spend some time asking God if there is a person from whom you've withheld forgiveness that you simply need to bless right now. You can sit right where you are and speak blessings over that person's life.

CLOSING PRAYER: As you reflect on just how much God has forgiven you, may you find yourself infused with the grace and strength through the power of Jesus Christ to forgive others.

BONUS ACTIVITY:

One of the most powerful movies exploring the themes of forgiveness and unforgiveness is *Les Miserable*. If you haven't seen the film, consider renting it this week.

DAY TWO

INEXHAUSTIBLE FORGIVENESS

BONUS ACTIVITY:

If you haven't read it yet, grab a copy of *The Hiding Place* from your local library or favorite bookstore. You'll be challenged in your faith.

ONE OF MY HEROES IS CORRIE TEN BOOM, author of *The Hiding Place*. In gripping terms, she describes the extreme abuses inflicted on her and other inmates in Nazi concentration camps during World War II as well as her personal journey after the war.

Sometime after Corrie was released, she began traveling through Europe speaking about the power of God's forgiveness and love.

After she taught in a church in Munich, a man approached her. She immediately recognized his face. He was one of the cruelest of her former guards. She stood breathless as he spoke of his newfound faith in Jesus. Then he extended his hand.

QUOTABLE:

"In him we have redemption through his blood, the forgiveness of sins, in accordance with the riches of God's grace that he lavished on us. With all wisdom and understanding, he made known to us the mystery of his will according to his good pleasure, which he purposed in Christ, to be put into effect when the times reach their fulfillment—to bring unity to all things in heaven and on earth under Christ." –Ephesians 1:7-10

"If you can forgive me, then I'll know what you say is true—that God forgives me."

Corrie felt pangs of anger and rage. She realized that though she'd been speaking to others about forgiveness, the scenes of the Nazi camp played in her mind like an unending movie reel.

Realizing that apart from forgiveness the movie reel would not stop, she began praying for the strength and grace to offer forgiveness she did not have. She stuck her hand out and clasped the former guard's.

In that moment, she says, something miraculous happened: "A current seemed to pass from me to him, while into my heart sprang a love for this stranger that almost overwhelmed me."[17]

Forgiveness is a gift that only God can infuse within us. I love that Corrie describes the experience as a "current" that passed between her and the former guard. Though inexplicable, God was at work filling her with a grace and compassion she did not have. We all need a current of forgiveness running through us.

The wonder of forgiveness is that when we forgive—we not only find freedom for ourselves but we extend the freedom to others. Sometimes I don't think we realize the power of forgiveness—in our lives, in the lives of others, and in our world.

How do you think the story would have ended differently if Corrie had refused to forgive or not asked God for the strength to forgive?

QUOTABLE:

"Forgiveness is the fragrance the violet sheds on the heel that has crushed it."
–George Roemisch, poet[18]

Corrie's story reminds me how much we all need to lean into God when we're struggling to forgive. I found this to be particularly true when I was trying to forgive Eugene Davidson, the man who embezzled us. For more than a year, Davidson had been my own personal Bernie Madoff. While Madoff developed a Ponzi scheme considered to be the largest financial fraud in U.S. history, Davidson developed a much smaller version. But those left in the wake still suffered the same.

I wanted to forgive him, but the scenes of what he'd done to us—the stress, the time, the angst, the loss—kept replaying in my mind. Every time I saw his name in an article or another notice from the IRS as a result of the money he stole, I could feel my blood pressure rise and muscles tighten.

In addition, the temptation to steal from others began raging in my life. I'd never been tempted by thievery before. The temptation seemed to come out of nowhere. I asked the Lord, "Where is this temptation coming from?"

Then one day, I stumbled on a story of a woman who had been sold into slavery. She spent years of her life performing sexual acts at the command of her captors. The police eventually freed her. With the help of a nonprofit organization, she secured an education and started a business to support the two young boys she had given birth to while in the sex industry.

Despite the incredible transformation that had taken place in her life, she admitted that some days she looked in the eyes of her own sons and felt an overwhelming desire to rape them. To resist the temptation, she had to fight with everything she had. I wanted to despise her except I understood her. She had been sexually abused and the temptation to sexually abuse others surged in her veins.

One of the ways the enemy exploits unforgiveness is by tempting us to take the wrong we've experienced and inflict it on someone else. This is one reason those who have been abused are often tempted to become abusers.

When have you been tempted to inflict a wrong done to you on someone else?

QUOTABLE:

"The LORD is compassionate and gracious, slow to anger, abounding in love. He will not always accuse, nor will he harbor his anger forever; he does not treat us as our sins deserve or repay us according to our iniquities. For as high as the heavens are above the earth, so great is his love for those who fear him; as far as the east is from the west, so far has he removed our transgressions from us." –Psalm 103:8-12

Yet despite my desire to forgive, saying "I forgive you" wasn't enough, especially after the months of turmoil we'd been through. I tried praying for Davidson and his family, but my heart still remained hard.

I needed to extend the kind of forgiveness Jesus described, an inexhaustible forgiveness, whose only condition is that we keep extending it again and again. I confessed to God that I didn't have the grace or strength to forgive Davidson on my own. I asked God to give me that which I did not have. I pursued forgiving Davidson as if it were a discipline, something I needed to do each and every day, rather than a one-time act.

Jesus once told Peter that he didn't need to forgive seven times, but seven times seventy. I have a hunch Jesus knew that sometimes that's how many times total forgiveness takes. For me, somewhere between number 372 and 379 I began to lose count and allow inexhaustible forgiveness into the deepest part of my heart. Soon after, any temptation to steal disappeared from my life.

Do you tend to think about forgiveness as a discipline or a one-time act?

QUOTABLE:

"When you release the wrongdoer from the wrong, you cut a malignant tumor out of your inner life. You set a prisoner free, but you discover that the real prisoner was yourself." –Lewis B. Smedes, author and theologian[19]

Who have you forgiven in the past where it required more than a one-time act?

Who do you need to forgive right now that will require you to embrace forgiveness as a discipline?

QUOTABLE:

"'Come now, let us settle the matter,' says the LORD. 'Though your sins are like scarlet, they shall be as white as snow; though they are red as crimson, they shall be like wool.'" –Isaiah 1:18

Something I discovered in the process of forgiving Davidson is how much we all need forgiveness—including me. The wrong Davidson committed reminded me of many of the wrongs I've committed both by what I've done and what I've left undone.

In forgiving Davidson, I was reminded that no one can know the full extent of our sins or the harm we've done to others. Yet even in the moments we can't bear to face the most horrible things we've done, or left undone, God still waits open-armed, ready to heal, restore, and forgive us.

Where have you struggled to accept God's forgiveness in your life?

I don't know who has hurt you deeply, but I do know the journey of forgiveness will look different for you. Like snowflakes, no two injuries are the same. The wounds and afflictions of life always differ, even in the tiniest degree, by factors such as timing, repetitiveness, sensitivity, and depth. Our wounds are compounded or lessened by our level of maturity and health. The words that penetrate the heart and scar one day can brush off without breaking the skin another. Regardless of the level of injury, Christ calls us to forgive. But we do not have to make the journey alone. We can ask God to provide the grace and strength to forgive and know that He will answer.

CLOSING PRAYER: Spend some time asking God to reveal any hidden areas of unforgiveness in your heart. Prayerfully consider any people who you may have tried to forgive as a one-time act, but now realize you need to commit to forgive them each day as a discipline.

DAY THREE

THE POWER OF BLESSING YOUR ENEMIES

WHEN LEIF AND I WERE FIRST MARRIED, we experienced those moments of miscommunication, misunderstanding, and frustration that naturally are compounded whenever a newlywed couple begins living together. We knew we were supposed to forgive, and we even had a theory that Ephesians 4:26—that passage about not letting the sun go down while you're still angry—was secretly inserted in the Bible just for us.

But despite all of my desire to forgive, I struggled to let issues go. Leif and I would miscommunicate. I'd say aloud that I forgave him, but in my heart I still pouted. The tinge of resentment remained. And it bothered me.

Can you relate to our experience? How have you struggled with forgiveness?

The remnants of unforgiveness were unpleasant, but I was concerned we were beginning to build an unhealthy pattern in our relationship early on. I prayed and asked God for wisdom. What could we do that would allow me to forgive more wholly and completely so we could move on quickly?

I remember reading in the Gospel of Luke where Jesus challenges us to bless those who curse us (Luke 6:28). I began exploring this idea of blessing our enemies throughout the Scripture and discovered passages including the following:

"Do not repay evil with evil or insult with insult. On the contrary, repay evil with blessing, because to this you were called so that you may inherit a blessing." –1 Peter 3:9

Reflecting on this and other passages, I suggested to Leif that whenever one of us acknowledged a wrong—whether one of us had committed or simply felt we'd been wronged—the person needing forgiveness had to ask, "Will you forgive me?"

The other person was free to say, "yes" or "Not right now—I need time."

Sometimes that "time" translated into a few minutes or a few hours to cool down. But as soon as the other person said, "Yes, I forgive you," they had to follow with three compliments about the other person.

Any kind expression counted. Things like, "I love being married to you." "I'm glad you picked me." "I love your generosity." "I appreciate the kindness you show others." "I'm grateful for your commitment to me." "I like cuddling with you."

What I discovered is that by the time I said or received three compliments, any residue of resentment was gone. The act of blessing or being blessed melted my hard heart. The pouting and lingering unforgiveness disappeared.

With whom in your life could you practice the Three Kind Words strategy in moments when forgiveness is required?

Over the course of the next week, consider practicing the Three Kind Words strategy with someone you know—a friend, a coworker, a roommate, a family member, or your spouse. Plan on sharing your stories about blessing those who wrong you in the final gathering.

CLOSING PRAYER: Spend some time asking God if there is a person from whom you've withheld forgiveness that you simply need to bless right now. You can sit right where you are and speak blessings over their life.

DAY FOUR

LAYING HOLD OF THE WONDER OF FORGIVENESS

SEVERAL YEARS AGO, a friend asked me what I'd like for my birthday. I told her a gift card to a specific store I love would be amazing. She purchased me a gift card to a different store. To be honest, I felt a little torn. I was grateful for the gift, but bewildered as to why she would ask what I wanted, then not purchase the item. I decided to overlook the matter and simply be thankful.

The following year, she gave me another gift for my birthday. Three months late. The gift was a certificate for something I don't like or enjoy. I was bothered more than grateful, which proved even more bothersome, because now I was annoyed with her and myself.

I realized my frustration wasn't about any of the birthday gifts, but a deeper issue in the relationship: I felt like my friend really didn't listen to me. Often when I spent time with her, I'd tell her openly and honestly what was going on in my life. The next time I saw her she didn't seem to have any recollection. As the months went by, I found myself pulling away from the relationship and a low-grade level of unforgiveness seeped into my heart. If honest, I was close to tossing the relationship away altogether.

The gift certificate merely brought the issue to light. I knew I needed to forgive her and also have an honest conversation about how I felt if I was going to strengthen the relationship. As I reflected on the situation, I realized that if I would have recognized and dealt with the unforgiveness sooner, the conversation I had to have would have been a lot easier.

In case you haven't noticed, the enemy loves to exploit unforgiveness wherever he can find it—in our relationships with our coworkers, church, each other, and God. The Adversary loves to take a small portion of unforgiveness and spread it as far and fast as he can. Maybe this is one reason Paul urges the believers in the

Corinthian church to forgive and keep forgiving.

Paul reminds his friends in Corinth that the church is the evidence of the Gospel in the world, but when unforgiveness festers in their hearts, they are allowing the enemy to work. Those who have been forgiven by Christ have no other choice but to forgive and not hold a grudge.

Why does Paul say forgiveness is essential in 2 Corinthians 2:5-11?

QUOTABLE:

"Probably more characters are spoiled by the nursing of grudges and the harbouring of grievances than by anything else." –R.V.G. Tasker, biblical scholar

When have you sensed the enemy exploiting an area of unforgiveness in your relationships? What was the result?

Sometimes unforgiveness doesn't only affect our individual relationships, but undermines an entire community.

When have you experienced Hebrews 12:15 to be true in your community?

We must be on the offensive when unforgiveness comes. We need to look for every opportunity to forgive and let go of the wrongs that have been done to us. Forgiveness has several components.

As you read the following facets of forgiveness, underline any phrases that catch your attention:

1 **ADMIT THE HURT.** Though we may be tempted to deny the pain, we need to acknowledge what's happened.

2 **CHOOSE AND COMMIT TO FORGIVE.** Forgiveness requires an active choice. But it's more than a one-time act. We must choose to forgive and commit to forgiving.

3 **TAKE OWNERSHIP OF WRONGDOING.** Forgiveness isn't just about letting go of what someone has done to us, but recognizing the wrong we've done to others.

4 **GIVE UP ALL RIGHTS.** Though the person has done something wrong, we need to be prepared to give up our right to retribution, our desire for vindication, and even our right to an apology.

5 **MOVE ON.** Though the memory of hurt may try to replay itself, we need to choose to press stop in our minds.

On the continuum below, mark how often you're tempted to meditate on the same offense over and over:

I play the offense in my mind repeatedly. — Once forgiven, it's forgotten.

When have you felt like a prisoner of unforgiveness?

Right now I'd like to invite you to take a few moments and ask the Holy Spirit to illuminate any people, situations, or organizations where you may be harboring unforgiveness unaware in your heart.

Before you begin, take a moment to reflect on all that God has forgiven you from the first day's homework from this session. Remember how and when God has forgiven you.

QUOTABLE:

"Apart from me you can do nothing." –John 15:5

Then spend 10 minutes asking God where you're harboring unforgiveness in your life. Ask God to bring names to mind where there's an element of unforgiveness. Don't rush through the time.

Write each name in the space below:

WITH EACH NAME LISTED, I'D LIKE YOU TO GO THROUGH THE FOLLOWING STEPS TOWARD FORGIVENESS.

STEP 1: Make a decision to forgive. Say the person's name aloud and verbally acknowledge the wrong or perceived wrong they've committed. It may help to say aloud, "I choose and commit to forgiving you through the grace and power of Jesus Christ who forgave me."

STEP 2: Ask God to reveal how one offense may have multiplied itself. Ask God to forgive you for any ways you contributed to the wrong, and ask God to forgive you for harboring the unforgiveness. If needed, ask God to give you the grace and strength to forgive yourself and God for allowing this wrong to happen.

STEP 3: Bless the person you're forgiving by speaking kind expressions as prayers for the person. Consider praying that God would bless the person in three specific ways.

As you go through these steps of forgiveness, ask God to give you courage and strength not only to forgive, but to live more freely as one who has been forgiven.

How does forgiving others make you feel freer?

BONUS ACTIVITY: I'd love to hear how God has been revealing Himself to you during this study. Would you be willing to drop me an e-mail at *wonderstruck@margaretfeinberg.com*? Your note will make my day!

With that friend I mentioned, I finally told her about how I was feeling. She apologized profusely and committed to make some changes in the relationship. And I agreed to extend her abundant grace and let her know any time I felt like I wasn't being heard. As a result, the relationship is stronger and better than it has ever been.

CLOSING PRAYER: Spend time thanking God for the work of forgiveness He's doing in and through you. Ask God to continue to strengthen your resolve to forgive and ask forgiveness from others.

DAY FIVE

WONDERSTRUCK IN YOUR EVERYDAY

TIME FLIES WHEN you're with someone you enjoy. I can't believe this is our last day together. I've been praying for you and the work God has been doing in you. Though I can't see your face or look into your eyes, know that with each lesson I've been asking God to meet you in a personal and profound way. I've been asking that you'll find yourself wonderstruck by one more glimpse of our marvelous God.

+ BONUS ACTIVITY:

Don't forget to continue adding moments where you've been wonderstruck by God in your Wonderstruck Journal.

I think it's appropriate in this final session that we reflect on the idea that God wants to give us moments of spiritual awakening in our everyday that make us desire to know Him more. Sometimes those moments are wildly profound.

In the Book of Exodus, Moses and the Israelites find themselves pinned up against the Red Sea. Pharaoh's army is chasing the people down to bring them back to slavery in Egypt. Yet in one of God's most miraculous displays, God reaches down and peels the sea open into two halves until the Israelites can make it safely to the other side. Then God releases the waters. The Egyptian army washes away.

Moses, Miriam, and the Israelites are wonderstruck. They've experienced an unforgettable moment of spiritual awakening that makes them want more of God. In response, they break out in a song of worship and adoration. They praise God for His strength and the source of their salvation. They recognize God is majestic in power and comparable to no other.

What do the Israelites discover to be true about God through their encounter with Him in Exodus 15:1-11?

What have you learned about God through the moments He revealed Himself in powerful ways in your life?

In what situations do you need to see a demonstration of God's power and majesty right now?

QUOTABLE:

"I will give thanks to you, LORD, with all my heart; I will tell of all your wonderful deeds." –Psalm 9:1

Sometimes we can convince ourselves that the miracles we read about in the Bible only happened way back then. We can tell ourselves that God doesn't want to split open seas today. But the same God who revealed Himself as Rescuer, Savior, and Protector to the Israelites wants to reveal Himself as the One who rescues, saves, and protects us today.

Take a moment to ponder the power, strength, holiness, and might of God. Reflect on the mystery that God not only created all things but holds all things together. Consider the limitless love God displayed when His only Son Jesus came to earth for what some might consider the real Mission: impossible.

Sometimes the way God reveals His wonder is far subtler. One of my favorite stories is an unsuspecting man whose main distinction in the Bible is that he carries a water pot.[18] The Scripture doesn't even say the water pitcher is particularly heavy or huge or decorated. Just a plain water pitcher.

Yet in making preparations for the celebration of the final Passover with the disciples, Jesus instructs several of His followers, "He sent two of His disciples and said to them, "Go into the city, and a man carrying a jar of water will meet you. Follow him" (Mark 14:13).

The man is likely inconvenienced and possibly embarrassed to carry such a water pitcher. Why? One Bible scholar notes that women were primarily responsible for going to the well and bringing water to the home:

> "The custom of carrying water in the Holy Land is ancient. However, it was and is the woman's job to go to the well or spring with a pitcher and carry water to [her] home. When the Gibeonites deceived Joshua (9:3-27), he judged them and made them servants to chop wood and carry water. This punishment may seem mild to us, but how humiliating it was to a man—carrying water in public—a woman's job! This helps us to better understand how easy it was for the disciples to identify the man carrying the water pot when Jesus sought an upper room [in which] to eat the Passover. It was not a question of seeking one man out of many carrying a water pot—this man would stick out above all others, in that he alone would be carrying one. A man may carry a water skin, but seldom does one carry a water pot."[20]

Yet the water pot was the very thing that God used to help the disciples recognize who they were to follow. The disciples followed the man into a house—the same house where Christ's final Passover was hosted.

What do you think is running through the man with the water pitcher's mind in Mark 14:12-16?

Sometimes I imagine the man huffing and puffing, upset he has to do such a low, menial task. I speculate that as a servant of the house, maybe he is having a bad day as he carries the plain water pitcher. My hunch is that he doesn't have a clue he is being used by God to lead the disciples to the upper room—a place they'd celebrate their final Passover with Christ, a place they'd soon wait for the promised Holy Spirit.

The miracle isn't only found in an unsuspecting man carrying a plain water pitcher, but the water he carries in the pitcher. Maybe the water is served to the disciples as they ate the Passover. Or maybe, just maybe, the water is used when Jesus washed the disciples' feet. On this side of heaven, we'll never know.

What we do know is that God chose to use an unsuspecting man carrying a plain water pitcher to lead the disciples on their way. And that leaves me wonderstruck. Because if God can use that man, then He can use anyone, anytime He fancies—including you and me.

Sometimes the way God reveals His wonder is shiny and sparkly and sometimes more subdued. My prayer for you throughout this *Wonderstruck* study is that you'll open your arms and eyes to the God who stands in plain sight and works miracles in your midst. That you'll experience God's presence and handiwork in ways you never have before. For when you search for God, you *will* discover Him.

As our time together comes to a close, I want to thank you for going on this adventure with me. I hope I can meet you one day and hear your story of how God allowed you to be wonderstruck.

Live awake and aware for the wonder awaits.

CLOSING PRAYER: Spend time in prayer and thanksgiving for the ways God has revealed His wonder to you over the last six sessions. Ask God to continue opening your eyes and heart to His presence all around.

FINAL CELEBRATION GATHERING

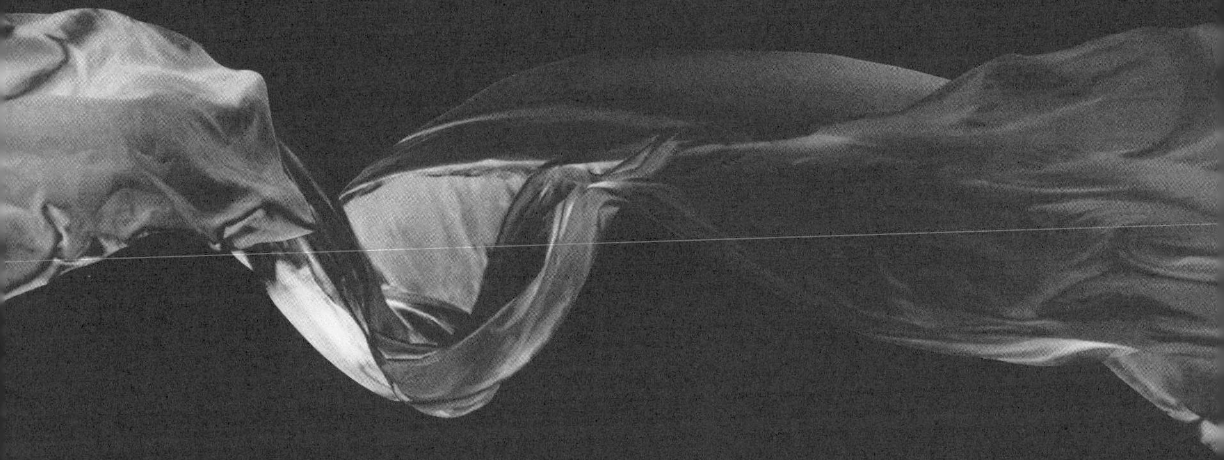

SESSION SEVEN

GROUP

SESSION SEVEN:
FINAL CELEBRATION

EXPERIENTIAL ACTIVITY: CELEBRATE THE WONDER OF GOD IN OUR LIVES

WHAT YOU'LL NEED:

- Each person to bring food to share
- Party balloons
- Fun decorations
- I've Been Wonderstruck By ... found on page 172
- Digital camera or cell phone with camera
- Blue or black marker

1 Decorate the room with balloons, streamers, wildflowers, and anything you can find to create a festive atmosphere.

2 Enjoy laughing, talking, sharing, and catching up as you eat together.

3 Invite participants to fill out the I've Been Wonderstruck By ... with a marker on page 173.

4 Take pictures of group members with their signs and send the photos to us at *wonderstruck@margaretfeinberg.com*. We'd love to post the pictures on our website.

5 Discuss the following questions:

- What activity could your group do together to bring the wonder of God to others?
- Is there a specific need in your community or church where your group can be of service, encouragement, or help?
- Don't just talk about a possible activity—commit to sharing God's love and many wonders with others today.

PLAY THE SESSION SEVEN VIDEO: [11:45]

NOTES

VIDEO DISCUSSION

1 Throughout this study you've been asked to make daily entries into the Wonderstruck Journal. Share three more moments in which you've encountered the wonder of God and His handiwork with the group.

2 In Day One's homework, you were challenged to practice the Three Kind Words strategy on someone during the course of the week. Who did you try to use the strategy with? What did you discover about blessing others who wrong you?

3 What aspect of Matthew 5:44-45 is most challenging for you? Why?

4 During Day Two's homework, you were asked to make a list of 30 things for which God has forgiven you. Why do you think it's so easy to forget how much you've been forgiven? How did creating the list strengthen your resolve to forgive others?

5 Day Three's homework challenged you to go through a specific exercise in order to identify areas of unforgiveness and begin forgiving and blessing those who have hurt or disappointed you. What did you learn or discover as you went through the exercise?

6 Margaret says that forgiveness can be more of a discipline than a one-time act. When have you found this to be true in your own life?

7 Reflecting on your time in this study, how does nurturing a sense of divine expectation and praying for wonder make you more sensitive to God in your everyday life?

CLOSING PRAYER

As you close in prayer ask:

- God to continue to awaken each person's heart, mind, and spirit to a sense of God's wonder
- God to continue revealing His character and presence in tangible ways to each person
- the Holy Spirit to continue creating opportunities to grow in faith and faithfulness as each person responds to our wondrous God.

THE WONDERSTRUCK JOURNAL

"Many, LORD my God, are the wonders you have done, the things you planned for us. None can compare with you; were I to speak and tell of your deeds, they would be too many to declare." —Psalm 40:5

Each day write down three wonders of God and His handiwork.

Here are a few to get you started:

- the scent of a newborn child
- partaking of the bread and the cup
- divine timing
- the wisdom of a child
- a fading sunset
- a word of kindness
- a meaningful Scripture
- the crunch of an almond
- an act of grace
- a much-needed rain

THE WONDERSTRUCK JOURNAL

THE WONDERSTRUCK JOURNAL

THE WONDERSTRUCK JOURNAL

THE WONDERSTRUCK JOURNAL

I'VE BEEN WONDERSTRUCK BY . . .

WHAT HAVE YOU BEEN WONDERSTRUCK BY? Follow the directions below and join others around the world in a photo collection that describes how God reveals Himself in our daily lives. Here's how:

FIRST...

- Write down your answer to "I've been wonderstruck by ..." on the following page. Or download more copies at margaretfeinberg.com/freegifts.

NEXT...

- Take a photo of yourself with your sign with a camera, cell phone, or webcam.

FINALLY...

- E-mail your photo to *wonderstruck@margaretfeinberg.com.*
- Share your photo on Margaret Feinberg's Facebook wall.
- Tweet and Instagram your photo using #livewonderstruck.
- Hang your answer around your house or workplace as a reminder of God's marvelous work in your life.

TIPS AND HINTS...

- There's no right or wrong answer. Feel free to use one of the responses from your Wonderstruck Journal.
- Use a large marker for readability.
- Be creative. Photos will be featured on Margaret's website, Facebook, and/or Twitter.

I'VE BEEN WONDERSTRUCK BY . . .

ENDNOTES

1. "Wonder," Dictionary.com [online, cited 22 Sept. 2012]. Available from the Internet: *http://dictionary.reference.com.*
2. Michael Card, *Luke: The Gospel of Amazement* (Downers Grove, IL: InterVarsity Press, 2011), 22.
3. This phrase, "First Amendment of the faithful," is used by Ellen F. Davis in her thought-provoking book, *Getting Involved with God: Rediscovering the Old Testament* (Cambridge: Cowley Publications) whose work I'm indebted to from my time of revisiting the Psalms.
4. Francis I. Anderson, *Tyndale Old Testament Commentary: Job* (Downers Grover, IL: InterVarsityPress, 2008), 67.
5. Frederick Buechner, *Wishful Thinking: A Seeker's ABC* (San Francisco: Harpers San Francisco, 1973), 57.
6. Thanks to Sam O'Neal, author of *Field Guide for Small Group Leaders,* for this idea.
7. "Sleep Deprivation," Sleepdex [online, cited 22 Sept. 2012]. Available from the Internet: *www.sleepdex.org/deficit.htm.*
8. John Ruskin, *Streams in the Desert* (Grand Rapids, MI: Zondervan, 1997), 44.
9. Frederick Buechner, *Wishful Thinking: A Seeker's ABC* (San Francisco: Harpers San Francisco, 1973), 85.
10. Stephen H. Shoemaker, *Finding Jesus in His Prayers* (Nashville: Abingdon Press, 2004), 40.
11. Kenneth E. Bailey, *Jesus Through Middle Eastern Eyes: Cultural Studies in the Gospels* (Downers Grove: InterVarsity Press, 2008), 119.
12. C.S. Lewis, *Letters to Malcolm: Chiefly on Prayer* (Orlando, FL: Harcourt, 1992), 106.
13. Darrell L. Bock, *NIV Application Commentary: Luke* (Grand Rapids, MI: Zondervan, 1996), 454.
14. C.S. Lewis, *The Four Loves* (Orlando, FL: Harcourt Brace & Co., 1988), 121.
15. "Forgive" in *The American Heritage Dictionary of the English Language,* Fourth Edition (Boston, MA: Houghton Mifflin Company, 2006).
16. Charles Stanley, *Landmines in the Path of the Believer* (Nashville: Thomas Nelson, 2007), 130.
17. Corrie Ten Boom, *The Hiding Place* (Grand Rapids, MI: Chosen Books, 1971), 247-248.
18. George Roemisch, "Forgiveness," as quoted in Abigail Van Buren, "Dear Abby: Invest in Forgiveness and Reap Its Benefits," *Chicago Tribune,* February 5, 1996, online. Available from *www.chicagotribune.com.*
19. Lewis B. Smedes, *Forgive and Forget: Healing the Hurts We Don't Deserve* (New York: HarperCollins Publishers, 1996), 133.
20. Robert Boyd, *World's Bible Handbook* (Iowa Falls, IA: World Bible Publishers, 1991), 122.

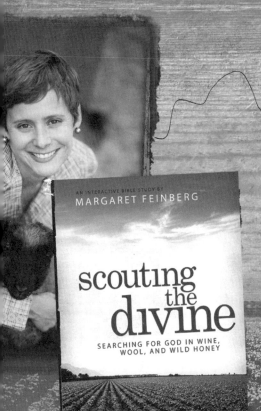

WONDERSTRUCK SCRIPTURE MEMORIZATION CARDS

Scripture memorization is a spiritual discipline useful for filling our minds with what our hearts need. Psalms 119:11 says, "I have hidden your word in my heart that I might not sin against you." When we memorize Scripture, it's easier to share the good news of Jesus, remain anchored in God's truth in difficult situations, and learn to meditate and delight in God's law (Psalm 1:2).

If you're like me, memorization doesn't always come easily. When spending time disciplining myself in Scripture memorization, I have to think of mnemonic games or tricks to get each verse or passage to stick. I encourage you to do the same. Here are a few helpful hints that may assist you as you memorize each session's verses:

- Choose a translation that is easiest for you to remember or one you are most familiar with.
- Practice by writing out the verse three times. Each time begin writing without looking.
- Spend time dissecting the verse and meaning using the surrounding verses and a commentary. Scripture memory is easier when the passage is fully understood.
- Read the verse aloud three times, then try to recite it without looking.
- Use Google to see if any worship songs have been written about the passage you're memorizing or make up your own song to practice reciting.
- Find an accountability partner with whom you can recite verses together.
- Set a goal date to have a certain Scripture memorized.
- Write out the Scripture on colorful pieces of paper or paint on a canvas with your favorite Pinterest materials. Hang the artwork around your home or workplace to be reminded of the verse often.
- Write out the individual words on different note cards, mix them up, then try and put the words back in order.
- Be sure to break down the verse you're memorizing into smaller chunks to make it easier to swallow.

Don't get discouraged! Scripture memorization is a discipline which requires practice. I hope the flash cards will be something you carry with you throughout the next six weeks as you begin the process of memorizing.